The Alcoholism
and Drug Abuse

CLIENT WORKBOOK

2
EDITION

The Alcoholism and Drug Abuse

CLIENT WORKBOOK

2 EDITION

ROBERT R. PERKINSON

Keystone Treatment Center,
Canton, South Dakota

Los Angeles | London | New Delhi
Singapore | Washington DC

Los Angeles | London | New Delhi
Singapore | Washington DC

FOR INFORMATION:

SAGE Publications, Inc.
2455 Teller Road
Thousand Oaks, California 91320
E-mail: order@sagepub.com

SAGE Publications Ltd.
1 Oliver's Yard
55 City Road
London EC1Y 1SP
United Kingdom

SAGE Publications India Pvt. Ltd.
B 1/I 1 Mohan Cooperative Industrial Area
Mathura Road, New Delhi 110 044
India

SAGE Publications Asia-Pacific Pte. Ltd.
33 Pekin Street #02-01
Far East Square
Singapore 048763

Printed in the United States of America

This book is printed on acid-free paper.

Acquisitions Editor: Kassie Graves
Editorial Assistant: Courtney Munz
Production Editor: Brittany Bauhaus
Copy Editor: Megan Markanich
Typesetter: C&M Digitals (P) Ltd.
Proofreader: Theresa Kay
Cover Designer: Bryan Fishman
Marketing Manager: Katie Winter
Permissions Editor: Adele Hutchinson

11 12 13 14 15 10 9 8 7 6 5 4 3 2 1

Contents

Introduction

Congratulations and welcome to treatment! You have made a monumental step in recovery. You can be proud of yourself. You can feel confident that treatment works. Ninety percent of patients who work this program stay clean and sober. You will get your life back if you change a few simple things. These are called the tools of recovery. This program is not hard; it's easy, but you must do your part. It's going to take some work.

The illness of addiction is not you. You don't have to feel bad about yourself. This illness is a disease that lives inside of your brain. You are not bad; the illness is bad. You will find that this illness has a life of its own, and it will fight for survival. It will do everything in its power to get you off track and get you back to the addiction. The illness is cunning, baffling, and powerful. It often works out of your awareness, and you must use healthy thoughts and behaviors to stay in recovery.

Addiction is a chronic brain disease. The brain has been hijacked by an illness. You must be disciplined and fight for your life. Ninety-five percent of untreated addicts die of their addiction; alcoholics die 26 years earlier than they would otherwise. You are in a life and death struggle, and the war will be played out inside of your mind, body, and spirit. You are in for a fight for your life, but you are not alone. We are going to fight with you.

There are three things that you can do that will bring the illness under control. These new behaviors may seem unnatural for you at first, but you must do them all. If you leave one of the tools out, your chances of recovery significantly decrease.

Let's briefly go over the tools so that you can begin to understand them. You have to do three things to stay clean and sober: (1) get honest, (2) go to 12-step meetings, and (3) get on a spiritual journey to a Higher Power of your own understanding.

You can be proud of yourself now because you have done something right. For a long time, you have been living a life full of pain and lies. Now you will step out in truth to help yourself and others. This treatment is not just about you; it's about helping other addicts. The best thing you can do for yourself is to help somebody else. Remember this when you are feeling bad. When this happens, go to a 12-step meeting, call someone in the program, or find someone else in treatment and ask them how they are doing. Tell them your story, and give them an opportunity to tell their story. There is nothing more powerful than your story: how it was, what happened, and how it is now. Know that the second you stopped the addictive behavior your brain started healing. You are healing as you read these words, and every day it gets better.

Chemical Use History

This exercise will help you to become more aware of how chemicals have affected your life and the lives of those around you. Using alcohol or any other mood-altering substance is considered to be chemical use. Answer the questions as completely as you can. It is time to get completely honest with yourself. Write down exactly what happened.

1. How old were you when you had your first drink? Describe what happened and how you felt.

   _____

   _____

   _____

   _____

   _____

2. List all of the drugs you have ever used and the age at which you first used each drug.

   _____

   _____

   _____

   _____

3. What are your drug-using habits? Where do you use? With whom? Under what circumstances?

_____

_____

_____

_____

_____

_____

4. Was there ever a period in your life when you used too much or too often? Give at least five examples.

1. _____

2. _____

3. _____

4. _____

5. _____

5. Has using chemicals ever caused a problem for you? Describe the problem or problems. Give at least five examples.

1. _____

2. _____

3. _____

4. _____

5. _____

6. When you were using, did you find that you used more or for a longer period of time than you had originally intended? Give at least five examples.

    1. _____

    2. _____

    3. _____

    4. _____

    5. _____

7. Do you have to use more of the chemical now to get the same effect? How much more than when you first started?

_____

_____

_____

_____

_____

8. Did you ever try to cut down on your use? Why did you try to cut down, and what happened to your attempt?

_____

_____

_____

_____

9. List at least five ways you tried to cut down. Did you change your beverage? Limit the amount ("I would only have three tonight")? Restrict your use to a certain time of day ("I would only drink after five o'clock")?

1. _____

2. _____

3. _____

4. _____

5. _____

10. Did you ever stop completely? What happened? Why did you start again?

_____

_____

_____

_____

_____

11. Did you spend a lot of time intoxicated or hungover?

_____

_____

_____

_____

12. Did you ever use while doing something dangerous, such as driving a car? Give at least five examples.

    1. _____

    2. _____

    3. _____

    4. _____

    5. _____

13. Were you ever so high or hungover that you missed work or school? Give at least five examples.

    1. _____

    2. _____

    3. _____

    4. _____

    5. _____

14. Did you ever miss family events or recreation because you were high or hungover? Give at least five examples.

    1. _____

    2. _____

    3. _____

    4. _____

    5. _____

15. Did your use ever cause family problems? Give at least five examples.

1. _____

2. _____

3. _____

4. _____

5. _____

16. Did you ever feel annoyed when someone talked to you about your drinking or use of drugs? Who was this person, and what did he or she say? Give at least five examples.

1. _____

2. _____

3. _____

4. _____

5. _____

17. Did you ever feel bad or guilty about your use? Give at least five examples.

1. _____

2. _____

3. _____

4. _____

5. _____

18. Did using ever cause you any psychological problems such as being depressed? Explain what happened.

_____

_____

_____

_____

19. Did using ever cause you any physical problems or make a physical problem worse? Give a few examples.

_____

_____

_____

_____

20. Did you ever have a blackout? How old were you when you had your first blackout? Give some examples of blackouts.

_____

_____

_____

_____

_____

21. Did YOU ever get sick because you got too intoxicated? Give at least five examples.

    1. _____

    2. _____

    3. _____

    4. _____

    5. _____

22. Did you ever have a real bad hangover? Give at least five examples about how you felt.

    1. _____

    2. _____

    3. _____

    4. _____

    5. _____

23. Did you ever get the shakes or suffer withdrawal symptoms when you quit using? Describe what happened physically, mentally, and spiritually to you when you stopped using your drug of choice.

_____

_____

_____

_____

_____

_____

24. Did you ever use chemicals to avoid symptoms of withdrawal? Give at least five examples of when you used a substance to control withdrawal symptoms.

1. _____

2. _____

3. _____

4. _____

5. _____

25. Have you ever sought help for your drug problem? When? Who did you see? Did the treatment help you? How?

_____

_____

_____

_____

_____

26. Why do you continue to use? Give 5 to 10 reasons.

1. _____

2. _____

3. _____

4. _____

5. _____

6. _____

7. _____

8. _____

9. _____

10. _____

27. Why do you want to stop using? Give at least 10 reasons.

1. _____

2. _____

3. _____

4. _____

5. _____

6. _____

7. _____

8. _____

9. _____

10. _____

28. Has alcohol or drug use ever affected your reputation? Describe what happened and how you felt.

_____

_____

_____

_____

29. Describe the feelings of guilt you have about your use. How do you feel about yourself?

_____

_____

_____

_____

_____

30. How has using affected you financially? Give at least five examples of how you wasted money in your addiction.

1. _____

2. _____

3. _____

4. _____

5. _____

31. Has your ambition decreased due to your use? Give a few examples.

_____

_____

_____

_____

_____

_____

32. Has your addiction changed how you feel about yourself? How do you feel when you are seeking the addiction or in withdrawal?

_____

_____

_____

_____

_____

33. Are you as self-confident as you were before? How has the addiction affected your faith in yourself?

_____

_____

_____

_____

34. List at least 10 reasons why you want treatment now.

1. _____

2. _____

3. _____

4. _____

5. _____

6. _____

7. _____

8. _____

9. _____

10. _____

35. List all of the chemicals you have used in the past 6 months.

_____

_____

_____

_____

_____

36. List how often and in what amounts you have used each chemical in the past 6 months.

_____

_____

_____

_____

37. List the life events that have been affected by your chemical use (e.g., school, marriage, job, children).

_____

_____

_____

_____

38. Have you ever had legal problems because of your use? List each problem.

_____

_____

_____

_____

_____

39. How has your addiction affected your relationship with your parents and other family members? List at least 10 reasons.

1. _____

2. _____

3. _____

4. _____

5. _____

6. _____

7. _____

8. _____

9. _____

10. _____

40. If you are in school, list at least five ways your addiction affected your school-work and relationships with teachers and school administrators.

1. _____

2. _____

3. _____

4. _____

5. _____

41. Have you ever lost a job or been suspended or expelled from school because of your use? Describe each time.

_____

_____

_____

_____

_____

_____

42. Do you want treatment for your chemical problem? List at least 10 reasons why.

1. _____

2. _____

3. _____

4. _____

5. _____

6. _____

7. _____

8. _____

9. _____

10. _____

I am in the _____.

_____ Precontemplation stage

_____ Contemplation stage

_____ Preparation stage

_____ Action stage

_____ Maintenance stage

Honesty

This is an exercise to help you get honest with yourself. In recovery, it is essential to tell the truth. As you will hear at every 12-step meeting, this is a program of rigorous honesty. "Those who do not recover are people who cannot or will not completely give themselves to this simple program, usually men and women who are constitutionally incapable of being honest with themselves" (Alcoholics Anonymous [AA], 2001, p. 58).

Why is it so important to be honest? Because dishonesty to self and others distorts reality. "Rigorous honesty is the most important tool in learning to live for today" (Narcotics Anonymous [NA], 1988, p. 92). You never will solve problems if you lie. You need to live in the facts. In sobriety, you must commit yourself to reality. This means accepting everything that is real.

People who are chemically dependent think that they cannot tell the truth. They believe that if they do, they will be rejected. The facts are exactly the opposite; unless you tell the truth, no one can accept you. People have to know you to accept you. If you keep secrets, then you never will feel known or loved. An old AA saying states, "We are only as sick as our secrets." If you keep secrets from people, then you never will be close to them.

You cannot be a practicing alcoholic or drug addict without lying to yourself. You must lie and believe the lies or else the illness cannot continue. The lies are attempts to protect you from the pain of the truth. If you had known the truth, then you would have known that you were sick and needed treatment. This would have been frightening, so you kept the truth from yourself and from others. "Let us face it; when we were using, we were not honest with ourselves" (NA, 1988, p. 27).

There are many ways you lied to yourself. This exercise will teach you exactly how you distorted reality, and it will start you toward a program of honesty. Answer each of the following questions as completely as you can.

1. *Denying:* You tell yourself or others, "I do not have a problem." Write down at least five examples of when you used this technique to avoid dealing with the truth.

    1. _____

    2. _____

    3. _____

    4. _____

    5. _____

2. *Minimizing:* You make the problem smaller than it really was. You might have told yourself, or someone else, that your problem was not that bad. You might have told someone that you had a couple of beers when you really had six. Write down at least five examples of when you distorted reality by making it seem smaller than it actually was.

1. _____

2. _____

3. _____

4. _____

5. _____

3. *Being hostile:* You become angry or make threats when someone confronts you about your chemical use. Give at least five examples.

1. _____

2. _____

3. _____

4. _____

5. _____

4. *Rationalizing:* You make an excuse. "I had a hard day." "Things are bad." "My relationship is bad." "My financial situation is bad." Give at least 10 examples of when you thought that you had a good reason to use chemicals.

1. _____

2. _____

3. _____

4. _____

5. _____

6. _____

7. _____

8. _____

9. _____

10. _____

5. *Blaming:* You shift the responsibility to someone else. "The police were out to get me." "My wife is overreacting." Give at least five examples of when you blamed someone else for a problem you caused.

1. _____

2. _____

3. _____

4. _____

5. _____

6. *Intellectualizing:* You overanalyze and overthink about a problem. You avoid doing something about it. "Sure I drink some, but everyone I know drinks." "I read this article, and it said that this is a drinking culture." Give at least five examples of how you use intellectual data and statistics to justify your use.

1. _____

2. _____

3. _____

4. _____

5. _____

7. *Diverting:* You bring up another topic of conversation to avoid the issue. Give at least five examples.

   1. _____

   2. _____

   3. _____

   4. _____

   5. _____

8. Make a list of five lies that you told to someone close to you about your drinking or drug use.

   1. _____

   2. _____

   3. _____

   4. _____

   5. _____

9. Make a list of five lies that you told yourself about your drug problem.

   1. _____

   2. _____

   3. _____

   4. _____

   5. _____

10. Make a list of 10 people you have lied to.

    1. _____

    2. _____

3. _____

4. _____

5. _____

6. _____

7. _____

8. _____

9. _____

10. _____

11. How do you feel about your lying? Describe at least five ways you feel about yourself when you lie.

1. _____

2. _____

3. _____

4. _____

5. _____

12. List five things you think will change in your life if you begin to tell the truth.

1. _____

2. _____

3. _____

4. _____

5. _____

13. List five ways you use lies in other areas of your life.

1. _____

2. _____

3. _____

4. _____

5. _____

14. When are you the most likely to lie? Is it when you have been drinking or using addictive behavior?

_____

_____

_____

_____

_____

15. Why do you lie? What does it get you? Give five reasons.

1. _____

2. _____

3. _____

4. _____

5. _____

16. Common lies of addiction are listed here. Give a personal example of each. Be honest with yourself.

A. Breaking promises:

_____

_____

_____

_____

B. Pretending to be clean and sober when you are not:

_____

_____

_____

_____

C. Pretending you remember things when you do not remember because of the addiction:

_____

_____

_____

_____

D. Minimizing use: Telling someone you drink or use no more than others use:

_____

_____

_____

_____

E. Telling yourself that you were in control when you were not:

_____

_____

_____

_____

F. Telling someone that you never have been involved in addictive behavior:

_____

_____

_____

_____

G. Hiding morning drinking:

_____

_____

_____

_____

H. Hiding your supply:

_____

_____

_____

_____

_____

I. Substituting the addiction for food or things you or your family needs:

_____

_____

_____

_____

J. Saying that you had the flu when you were really hungover or sick from the addiction:

_____

_____

_____

_____

K. Having someone else call into work to say that you are too sick to come to work:

_____

_____

_____

L. Pretending not to care about your addiction:

_____

_____

_____

_____

_____

People who are addicted lie to avoid facing the truth. Lying makes them feel more comfortable, but in the long run they end up feeling isolated and alone. Recovery demands living in the truth. "I am an alcoholic or an addict." "My life is unmanageable." "I am powerless over alcohol." "I need help." "I cannot do this alone." All of these are honest statements from someone who is living in reality.

Either you will get real and live in the real world or you will live in a fantasy world of your own creation. If you get honest, then you will begin to solve real problems. You will be accepted for who you are.

Wake up tomorrow morning and promise yourself that you are going to be honest for the next hour. Then try it for a half day and then whole day. Stop and check your feelings, and write down five ways you feel different when you are honest.

Write down in a diary when you are tempted to lie. Watch your feelings when you lie. How does it feel? How do you feel about yourself? Keep a list of five ways you feel different about yourself when you lie. Keep a diary for 5 days, and share it with your group or counselor. Tell them why you lied and how you felt about yourself when you lied. Then tell the group or counselor how it feels to be honest.

Take a piece of paper and write the word *truth* on it; then tape it to your bathroom mirror. Commit yourself to rigorous honesty. You deserve to live a life filled with love and truth. You never need to lie again.

I am in the _____.

_____ Precontemplation stage

_____ Contemplation stage

_____ Preparation stage

_____ Action stage

_____ Maintenance stage

Step One

We admitted that we were powerless over alcohol—that our lives had become unmanageable.

—Alcoholics Anonymous (AA) (2001, p. 59)

Before beginning this exercise, please read Step One in *Twelve Steps and Twelve Traditions* (AA, 2002).

No one likes to admit defeat. Our minds rebel at the very thought that we have lost control. We are big, strong, intelligent, and capable. How can it be that we are powerless? How can it be that our lives are unmanageable? This exercise will help you to sort through your life and make some important decisions. Answer each question that applies to you as completely as you can. This is an opportunity for you to get accurate. You need to see the truth about yourself.

Let us pretend for a moment that you are the commander in a nuclear missile silo. You are in charge of a 10-megaton bomb. If you think about it, this is exactly the kind of control you want over your life. You want to be in control of your thinking, feeling, and behavior. You want to be in control all of the time, not just some of the time. If you do something by accident or do something foolishly, you might kill many people. You never want to be out of control of your behavior, not even for a second.

People who are powerless over alcohol or drugs occasionally will be under the influence of the chemical when they are doing something physically hazardous. They may be intoxicated or hungover when they are working, using dangerous equipment, or driving. More than 40,000 Americans are killed each year in alcohol-related accidents. If you have ever done anything like this, then you have been out of control. You have risked your own life and the lives of others. Surely you cannot drive better when you are intoxicated than when you are sober. Now it is time to get honest with yourself.

POWERLESSNESS

1. Have you ever been intoxicated when you were doing something dangerous? For example, have you ever driven a car when you were using? Give five examples.

    1. _____

    2. _____

3. _____

4. _____

5. _____

Did you think that you were placing your life and the lives of others in jeopardy? What were you thinking?

_____

_____

_____

_____

_____

2. Whose lives did you risk? Make a list of 10 people you endangered.

1. _____

2. _____

3. _____

4. _____

5. _____

6. _____

7. _____

8. _____

9. _____

10. _____

How do you feel about putting all of those lives at risk?

_____

_____

_____

_____

_____

People who are powerless occasionally will do things while intoxicated or hungover that they feel bad or guilty about later. They might act foolishly at a party, act out sexually, get angry, or say things they do not mean. Have you ever done anything while intoxicated that you felt guilty or bad about later? Make a list of five things that made you feel the most uncomfortable. Be specific about what happened.

1. _____

2. _____

3. _____

4. _____

5. _____

People who are powerless gradually will lose respect for themselves. They will have difficulty in trusting themselves. In what ways have you lost respect for yourself due to drug or alcohol use?

1. _____

2. _____

3. _____

4. _____

5. _____

People who are powerless will do things that they do not remember doing. If you drink enough or use enough drugs, you cannot remember things properly. You might have people come up to you after a party and tell you something you did that you do not remember doing. You might wake up and not know where you are. You might not remember how you got home. This is a blackout, and it is very scary. You could have done anything. Most blackouts last a few minutes, but some can go on for hours or days.

1. Describe any blackouts you have had. Be specific about what you were doing and what happened.

_____

_____

_____

_____

2. How does it feel to know that you did something that you do not remember?

_____

_____

_____

_____

3. Think for a minute of what you could have done. You could have done anything and forgotten it.

_____

_____

_____

_____

_____

People who are powerless cannot keep promises that they make to themselves or others. They promise that they will cut down on their drinking, and they do not. They promise that they will not use, and they do. They promise to be home, to be at work, to be at the Cub Scout meeting, or to go to school, but they do not make it. They cannot always do what they want to do because sometimes they are too intoxicated or hungover. They disappoint themselves, and they lose trust in themselves. Other people lose trust in them. They can count on themselves some of the time, but they cannot count on themselves all of the time.

1. Did you ever promise yourself that you would cut down on your drug or alcohol use?

   Yes   No

2. What happened to these promises?

   _____

   _____

   _____

   _____

   _____

3. Did you ever promise yourself that you would quit entirely?

   Yes   No

4. What happened to your promise?

   _____

   _____

   _____

   _____

_____

_____

_____

5. Did you ever make a promise to someone that you did not keep because you were intoxicated or hungover? Give a few examples.

_____

_____

_____

_____

6. Are you reliable when you are intoxicated?

Yes   No

People who are powerless have accidents. They fall down or have accidents with their cars when they are intoxicated. Evidence proves that drugs profoundly affect thinking, coordination, and reaction time. Have you ever had an accident while intoxicated? Describe each accident in detail.

_____

_____

_____

_____

_____

People who are powerless lose control of their behavior. They do things that they would not normally do when they are clean and sober. They might get into fights. They might hit or yell at people they love—a spouse, child, parent, or friend. They might say things that they do not mean.

Have you ever gotten into a fight when you were intoxicated? Describe each instance, and describe what happened.

_____

_____

_____

_____

_____

People who are powerless say things that they do not mean. They might say sexual or angry things that they feel bad about later. They might not remember everything they said, but the other people do remember. Have you ever said something you did not mean while intoxicated? What did you say? What did you do?

_____

_____

_____

_____

People are powerless when they have feelings that they cannot deal with. They might drink or use drugs because they feel frightened, angry, or sad. They medicate their feelings. Have you ever used drugs to cover up your feelings? Give a few examples.

_____

_____

_____

_____

What feelings do you have difficulty coping with?

_____

_____

_____

_____

_____

People are powerless when they are not safe. List 10 reasons why you can no longer use drugs or alcohol.

1. _____

2. _____

3. _____

4. _____

5. _____

6. _____

7. _____

8. _____

9. _____

10. _____

People are powerless when they know that they should do something but they cannot do it. They may make a great effort, but they just cannot seem to finish what they started out to do.

1. Could you cut down on your drug or alcohol use every time you wanted and for as long as you wanted?

   Yes   No

2. Did being intoxicated or hungover ever keep you from doing something at home that you thought you should do? Give a few examples.

   _____

   _____

_____

_____

_____

3. Did being intoxicated or hungover ever keep you from going to work? Give a few examples.

_____

_____

_____

_____

4. Did you ever lose a job because of your drinking or drug use? Write down exactly what happened.

_____

_____

_____

_____

People are powerless when other people have to warn them that they are in trouble. You may have felt as if you were fine, but people close to you noticed that something was wrong. It probably was difficult for them to put their finger on just what was wrong, but they were worried about you. It is difficult to confront someone when the person is wrong, so people avoid doing so until they cannot stand the behavior anymore. When addicts are confronted with their behavior, they feel annoyed and irritated. They want to be left alone with the lies that they are telling themselves. Has anyone ever talked to you about your drinking or drug use? Who? How did you feel?

_____

_____

_____

_____

_____

People are powerless when they do not know the truth about themselves. Addicts lie to themselves about how much they are drinking or using. They lie to themselves about how often they use. They lie to themselves about their problems, even when the problems are obvious. They blame others for their problems. Here are some common lies they tell themselves:

"I can quit anytime I want to."

"I only had a couple."

"The police were out to get me."

"I only use when I need it."

"Everybody does it."

"I was drinking, but I was not drunk."

"Anybody can get arrested for drunk driving."

"My friends will not like me if I do not use."

"I never have problems when I drink beer."

"I will not drink until after 5 o'clock."

"From now on, I would only smoke pot."

"I am going to cut down to five pills a day."

Addicts continue to lie to themselves to the very end. They hold on to their delusional thinking, and they believe that their lies are the truth. They deliberately lie to those close to them. They hide their use. They make their problems seem smaller than they actually are. They make excuses for why they are using. They refuse to see the truth.

1. Have you ever lied to yourself about your chemical use? List 10 lies you told yourself.

   1. _____

   2. _____

3. _____

4. _____

5. _____

6. _____

7. _____

8. _____

9. _____

10. _____

2. List five ways in which you tried to convince yourself that you did not have a problem.

1. _____

2. _____

3. _____

4. _____

5. _____

3. List five ways in which you tried to convince others that you did not have a problem.

1. _____

2. _____

3. _____

4. _____

5. _____

UNMANAGEABILITY

Imagine that you are the manager of a large corporation. You are responsible for how everything runs. If you are not a good manager, then your business will fail. You must carefully plan everything and carry out those plans well. You must be alert. You must know exactly where you are and where you are going. These are the skills you need to manage your life effectively.

Chemically dependent persons are not good managers. They keep losing control. Their plans fall through. They cannot devise and stick to things long enough to see a solution. They are lying to themselves, so they do not know where they are and they are too confused to decide where they want to go next. Their feelings are being medicated, so they cannot use their feelings to give them energy and direction for problem solving. Problems are not solved; they escalate.

You do not have to be a bad manager all of the time to be a bad manager. It is worse to be a bad manager some of the time. It is very confusing. Most chemically dependent persons have flurries of productive activity when they work too much. They work themselves to the bone, and then they let things slide. It is like being on a roller coaster. Sometimes things are in control; sometimes things are out of control. Things are up and down, and they never can predict which way things are going to be tomorrow.

People's lives are unmanageable when they have plans fall apart because they were too intoxicated or hungover to complete them. Make a list of the plans you failed to complete because of your chemical use.

People's lives are unmanageable when they cannot manage their finances consistently.

1. List the money problems you are having.

_____

_____

_____

_____

_____

2. Are any of these problems the result of your addiction? Explain how chemicals have contributed to the problems.

_____

_____

_____

_____

_____

People's lives are unmanageable when they cannot trust their own judgment.

Have you ever been so intoxicated that you did not know what was happening? Explain.

_____

_____

_____

_____

Did you ever lie to yourself about your chemical use? Explain how your lies contributed your being unable to manage your life.

_____

_____

_____

_____

Have you ever made a decision while intoxicated that you were sorry about later? Explain.

_____

_____

_____

_____

_____

People's lives are unmanageable if people cannot work or play normally. Addicts miss work and recreational activities because of their drug use. They make excuses, but the real reason that they missed these events was they were too intoxicated or hungover.

Have you ever missed work because you were too intoxicated or hungover? List at least five times.

1. _____

2. _____

3. _____

4. _____

5. _____

Have you ever missed recreational or family activities because you were too drunk or hungover? List at least five times.

1. _____

2. _____

3. _____

4. _____

5. _____

People's lives are unmanageable if they are in trouble with other people or society. Chemically dependent persons will break the rules to get their own way. They have problems with authority.

Have you ever been in legal trouble when you were drinking or using drugs? Describe the legal problems that you have had.

_____

_____

_____

_____

_____

Have you ever had problems with your parents because of your drinking or using drugs? Explain.

_____

_____

_____

_____

Have you ever had problems in school because of your chemical use? Explain.

_____

_____

_____

_____

People's lives are unmanageable if people cannot consistently achieve their goals. Chemically dependent people reach out for what they want, but something keeps getting in the way. It does not seem fair. They keep falling short of their goals. Finally, they give up completely. They may have had the goal of going to school, getting a better job, improving their family problems, getting in good physical condition, or going on a diet. No matter what the goals are, something keeps going wrong. Chemically dependent people always will try to blame other people, but they cannot work hard enough or long enough to reach their goals. Alcoholics and drug addicts are good starters, but they are poor finishers.

List 10 goals that you had for yourself that you did not achieve due to the addiction.

1. _____

2. _____

3. _____

4. _____

5. _____

6. _____

7. _____

8. _____

9. _____

10. _____

People's lives are unmanageable if people cannot use their feelings appropriately. Feelings give us energy and direction for problem solving. Chemically dependent people medicate their feelings with drugs or alcohol. The substance gives them a different feeling—a chemically induced feeling. Chemically dependent people become very confused about how they feel.

What feelings have you tried to cope with addictive behavior?

_____

_____

_____

_____

_____

What feelings are created by your drug of choice? How do you feel when you are intoxicated or hungover?

_____

_____

_____

_____

People's lives are unmanageable if they violate their own rules, morals, and values. Chemically dependent persons compromise their values to continue using chemicals. They have the value not to lie, but they lie anyway. They have the value not to steal, but they steal anyway. They have the value to be loyal to their spouses or friends, but when they are intoxicated or hungover, they do not remain loyal. Their values and morals fall away, one by one. They end up doing things that they do not believe in. They know that they are doing the wrong thing, but they do it anyway.

Did you ever lie to cover up your addictive behavior? How did you feel about yourself?

_____

_____

_____

_____

_____

Were you ever disloyal to friends or family when using chemicals? List five times and discuss exactly what happened and how you felt about yourself.

1. _____

2. _____

3. _____

4. _____

5. _____

Did you ever steal to get your drugs? Explain what you did and how you felt about yourself later.

_____

_____

_____

_____

_____

Did you ever break the law when intoxicated? Exactly what did you do?

_____

_____

_____

_____

_____

Did you ever hit or hurt someone you loved while intoxicated or hungover? Explain each time in detail.

_____

_____

_____

_____

Did you treat yourself poorly by refusing to stop drinking or using drugs? Explain how you were feeling about yourself.

_____

_____

_____

_____

_____

Did you stop going to church? How did the make you feel about yourself?

_____

_____

_____

_____

_____

_____

People's lives are unmanageable when they continue to do things that give them problems. Chemicals create headaches, ulcers, nausea, vomiting, cirrhosis, and many other physical problems. Even if chemically dependent persons are aware of physical problems caused by chemicals, they keep on using anyway.

Chemicals cause psychological problems. They can make people feel depressed, fearful, anxious, or overly angry. Even if addicts are aware of these symptoms, they will continue to use.

Chemicals create relationship problems. They cause family problems such as family fights and verbal and physical abuse. They cause interpersonal conflicts at work, with family, and with friends. Chemically dependent persons withdraw and become more isolated and alone. Even if they believe that the problems are caused by the alcohol or drugs, they continue to use.

Did you have any persistent physical problems that were caused by your chemical use? Describe each problem.

_____

_____

_____

_____

_____

_____

Did you have any persistent psychological problems, such as anger, fear, hurt, depression, that were caused by your chemical use? Describe each problem in detail.

_____

_____

_____

_____

_____

Did you have persistent interpersonal conflicts that were made worse by your chemical use? Describe each problem in detail.

_____

_____

_____

_____

You must have good reasons to work toward a clean and sober lifestyle. Look over this exercise and list 10 reasons why you want to continue to remain clean and sober.

1. _____

2. _____

3. _____

4. _____

5. _____

6. _____

7. _____

8. _____

9. _____

10. _____

Make a list of these 10 things, and carry them around with you until you memorize them. Then when you think about becoming involved in the addiction again repeat the list over to yourself 10 times. After completing this exercise, take a long look at yourself.

1. I am powerless over my addiction.

    Yes   No

2. When I am involved in addictive behavior, my life becomes unmanageable.

    Yes   No

I am in the _____.

_____ Precontemplation stage

_____ Contemplation stage

_____ Preparation stage

_____ Action stage

_____ Maintenance stage

Step Two

[We] came to believe that a power greater than ourselves could restore us to sanity.

—Alcoholics Anonymous (AA) (2001, p. 59)

Before beginning this exercise, please read Step Two in *Twelve Steps and Twelve Traditions* (AA, 2002).

In Step One, you admitted that you were powerless over drugs or alcohol and that your life was unmanageable. In Step Two, you need to see the insanity of your disease and seek power to help you. If you are powerless, then you need power. If your life is unmanageable, then you need a manager. Step Two will help you to decide who that manager can be.

Most alcoholics and drug addicts who see the phrase *restore to sanity* revolt. They think that they may have a drinking or drug problem, but they do not feel as though they have a mental illness. They do not think that they have been insane.

In 12-step programs, the word *sanity* means being of sound mind. Someone with a sound mind knows what is real and knows how to adapt to reality. A sound mind feels stable, safe, and secure. Someone who is insane cannot see reality and is unable to adapt. A person does not have to have all of his or her reality distorted to be in trouble. If you miss a significant part of the journey ahead of you, then you will get lost. It only takes one wrong turn to end up in the ditch.

Going through life is like going on a long journey. You have a map given to you by your parents and significant others. The map shows the way to be happy and live your life in full. If you make significant wrong turns along the way, then you will end up unhappy and live an unfulfilling life. This is what happens in addiction. Searching for happiness, you make wrong turns. You think the addiction helps you to be and to feel better, but later you find out that this map is defective. Even if you followed your old map to perfection, you still would be lost. What you need is a new map. When you engage in addictive behavior the brain always says, "Good choice." Later you find the addiction has trapped you into a life full of incredible pain. Using this map, you have lost everything you wanted and broken every one of your own rules, morals, and values. The addiction has hijacked your brain, and you cannot say no to the addictive behavior or substance. Even in the face of profound negative consequences, you keep doing what you hate doing. You promise yourself that you will stop and get on a new road, but every time you try, you find yourself back to the old

51

road, the old map, the addiction. You are blocked in, lost, desperate, helpless, hope-less, and trapped. You find yourself in a muddy ditch, and the harder you try to get out the deeper you sink in.

Twelve-step programs give you a new map. It puts up 12 signposts to show the way. If you follow this map as millions of people have done, then you will find the joy and happiness that you have been seeking. You have reached and passed the first sign-post, Step One. You have decided that your life is powerless and unmanageable. Now you need a new source of power. You need someone else to help you get out of the ditch. You need to find some other person who can manage your life.

This is a spiritual program, and it directs you toward a spiritual answer to your prob-lems. It is not a religious program. Spirituality is the intimate relationship you have with yourself and all else. Religion is an organized system of faith and worship. Everyone has spirituality, but not everyone has religion.

You need to explore three relationships very carefully in Step Two: (1) the relation-ships with yourself, (2) the relationships with others, and (3) your relationship with a Higher Power. This Higher Power can be any Higher Power of your choice. If you do not have a Higher Power right now, do not worry. Most of us started that way. Just be willing to consider that there is a power greater than yourself in the universe.

To explore these relationships, you need to see the truth about yourself. If you see the truth, then you can find the way. First, you must decide whether you were insane. Did you have a sound mind or not? Let us look at this issue carefully.

People do not have a sound mind when they cannot remember what they did. They have memory problems. They do not have to have memory problems all of the time—just some of the time. People who abuse chemicals might not remember what hap-pened to them last night when they were intoxicated. Gamblers can lose hours of time without knowing the amount of time that has gone by. They can even gamble for 24 hours and think they just got to the casino. Alcoholics can wake up in another town or not know where they parked their car.

List any blackouts or memory problems you have had while being involved in your addictive behavior. You might have to think hard because you forgot, but if you try you can remember when you lost, time, money, or cannot remember some event. Try to list five times, and be as specific as you can.

1. _____

2. _____

3. _____

4. _____

5. _____

People who are insane lose control over their behavior. They do things when they are intoxicated or addicted that they never would do when they are sober.

List three times when you lost control over your behavior when intoxicated.

1. _____

2. _____

3. _____

List three times when you could not control your addictive behavior. You used more or longer than you intended.

1. _____

2. _____

3. _____

People who are insane consider self-destruction.
Did you ever consider hurting yourself when you were depressed about your addictive behavior?

Yes   No

Describe in detail what happened.

_____

_____

_____

_____

People who are insane feel emotionally unstable.
Have you ever thought that you were going crazy?

Yes   No

Describe this time.

_____

_____

_____

_____

_____

Have you felt emotionally unstable recently?

     Yes   No

Describe how you have been feeling about yourself and what you have done to those that have tried to love you.

_____

_____

_____

_____

_____

People who are insane are so confused that they cannot get their lives in order. They may frantically try to fix things, but problems stay out of control.

List five personal, family, work, or school problems that you have not been able to control.

1. _____

2. _____

3. _____

4. _____

5. _____

People who are insane cannot see the truth about what is happening to them. People who are addicted hide their addictive behavior from themselves and from others. They minimize, rationalize, and deny that there are problems.

Do you believe that you have been completely honest with yourself about your addiction?

     Yes   No

List 10 lies that you have told yourself.

1. _____

2. _____

3. _____

4. _____

5. _____

6. _____

7. _____

8. _____

9. _____

10. _____

People who are insane cut themselves off from healthy relationships. They might find that they do not communicate with significant others as well as they used to. They do not see their friends as often. They feel uncomfortable answering the phone, a knock at the door, or opening the mail. More and more of their lives center on the addiction.
List three people who you have stopped seeing.

1. _____

2. _____

3. _____

As your drinking and drug use increased, did you go to church less often?

Yes   No

List five relationships you have damaged in your drinking and drug use.

1. _____

2. _____

3. _____

4. _____

5. _____

People who are insane cannot deal with their feelings. Alcoholics and drug addicts cannot deal with their feelings. They do not like how they feel, so they medicate their feelings. They may drink or use drugs to feel less afraid or sad. They may drink to feel more powerful or more social.

List five feelings that you tried to change by drinking or using drugs.

1. _____

2. _____

3. _____

4. _____

5. _____

Now look back over your responses. Get out your Step One exercise and read it. Look at the truth about yourself. Look carefully at how you were thinking, feeling, and behaving when you were drinking, gambling, or using drugs. Make a decision. Do you think when you were involved in your addictive behavior that you had a sound mind? If you were unsound at least some of the time, then AA and Narcotics Anonymous (NA) would say you were insane. If you believe this to be true, then say this to yourself: "I am powerless. My life is unmanageable. My mind is unsound. I have been insane."

A POWER GREATER THAN OURSELVES

Consider a power greater than yourself. What exists in the world that has greater power than you do—a river, the wind, the universe, the sun?

List five things that have greater power than you do.

1. _____

2. _____

3. _____

4. _____

5. _____

The first Higher Power that you need to consider is the power of the group. The group is more powerful than you are. Ten hands are more powerful than two are. Two heads are better than one. AA and NA operate in groups. The group works like a family. The group process is founded in love and trust. All members share their experiences, strengths, and hopes in an attempt to help themselves and others. There is an atmosphere of anonymity. What you hear in group is confidential.

The group acts as a mirror reflecting you to yourself. The group members will help you to discover the truth about who and what you are. You have been deceiving yourself for a long time. The group will help you to uncover the lies. You will come to understand the old AA saying: "What we cannot do alone, we can do together." In group, you will have greater power over the disease because the group will see the whole truth better than you can. They will give you a new map, and this map will lead you to a new life full of happiness, joy, and peace.

You were not lying to hurt yourself. You were lying to protect yourself. In the process of building your lies, you cut yourself off from others and reality. This is how addiction works. You cannot recover from addiction by yourself. You need power coming from somewhere else. Begin by trusting your group.

- **Keep an open mind.**

You need to share in your group. The more you share, the closer you will get, and the closer you get, the more you can share. If you take risks and share your experience, strength, and hope then you will reap the rewards. You do not have to tell group everything, but you need to share as much as you can. The group can help you to straighten out your thinking and can help restore you to sanity.

Many chemically dependent persons are afraid of a Higher Power. They believe that a Higher Power will punish them or treat them in the same way as their fathers did. They might fear losing control. List five fears that you have about connecting with a Higher Power.

1. _____

2. _____

3. _____

4. _____

5. _____

Some chemically dependent persons have difficulty in trusting anyone. They have been so hurt by others that they do not want to take the chance of being hurt again. List five things that have happened in your life that make it difficult for you to trust others.

1. _____

2. _____

3. _____

4. _____

5. _____

What are at least five things that you will need to see from a Higher Power that will show you that the Higher Power can be trusted?

1. _____

2. _____

3. _____

4. _____

5. _____

Who was the most trustworthy person you ever knew?

Name:

How did this person treat you?

_____

_____

_____

_____

_____

How did you learn to trust him or her?

_____

_____

_____

_____

_____

List five things you hope to gain by accepting a Higher Power.

1. _____

2. _____

3. _____

4. _____

5. _____

AA wants you to come to believe in a power greater than yourself. You can accept any Higher Power that you feel can restore you to sanity. Your group, your counselor, your sponsor, and nature all can be used to give you this restoration. You must pick this Higher Power carefully. It is suggested that you use AA or NA as your Higher Power for now. Here is a group of millions of people who are recovering. They have found the way.

This program will direct you toward some sort of a God of your own understanding. The Big Book states, "That we were alcoholic and could not manage our own lives. That probably no human power could have removed our alcoholism. That God could and would if He were sought" (AA, 2001, p. 60).

Millions of chemically dependent persons have recovered because they were willing to reach out for God. AA makes it clear that nothing else will remove the obsession to use chemicals. Some of us have so glorified our own lives that we have shut out God. Now you have a new opportunity and a new need. You have a choice and you need a manager. You are at a major turning point. You can try to open your heart and let God in, or you can try to keep God out.

Remember that this is the beginning of a new life. To be new, you have to do things differently. All that the program is asking you to do is to be open to the possibility that there is a power greater than you are. AA does not demand that you believe in anything. The 12 steps are but suggestions. You do not have to accept all of this now, but you need to be open-minded and willing. Most recovering persons take Step Two a piece at a time.

First, you need to learn how to trust yourself. You must learn how to treat yourself well. What are five things you need to see from yourself that will show you that you are trustworthy?

1. _____

2. _____

3. _____

4. _____

5. _____

Then you need to try to trust your group. See whether the group members act consistently in your interest. They will not always tell you what you want to hear. No real friend would do that. They will give you the opportunity and encourage you to grow. What are at least five things you need to see from the group members that will show you that they are trustworthy?

1. _____

2. _____

3. _____

4. _____

5. _____

Every person has a unique spiritual journey. No one can start this journey with a closed mind. What is it going to take from God to show you that God exists? List as many as you can think of.

_____

_____

_____

_____

Step Two does not mean that we believe in God as God is presented in any religion. Remember that religion is an organized system of worship. Religion is created by humans. Worship means assigning worth to something. Many people have been so turned off by religion that the idea of God is unacceptable. Describe the religious environment of your childhood. What was it like? What did you learn about God from your parents, friends, or culture?

_____

_____

_____

_____

How did these early experiences influence the beliefs you have today?

_____

_____

_____

_____

What experiences have caused you to doubt God?

_____

_____

_____

_____

Your willingness is essential to your recovery. Give some examples of your willingness to trust in a Higher Power of your choice. What are you willing to do to try to be open-minded about a relationship with a Higher Power?

_____

_____

_____

_____

_____

Describe your current religious beliefs.

_____

_____

_____

_____

_____

Explain the God of your own understanding.

_____

_____

_____

_____

_____

List five reasons why a Higher Power will be good for you.

1. _____

2. _____

3. _____

4. _____

5. _____

If you asked the people in your AA/NA group to describe a Higher Power, you would get a variety of answers. Each person has his or her own understanding of a Higher Power. It is this unique understanding that allows a Higher Power to work individually for each of us. God comes to each of us differently.

The God shown to us in Scripture knows that love necessitates freedom. God created you and gave you the freedom to make your own decisions. You can do things that God does not want you to do. If God placed his face in the sky or was so obvious that everyone worshipped him, then no one would have a free choice. This is why God exists in a gentle whisper inside of your thoughts. You have to stop and listen to hear God. It is incredibly easy to keep God out, and it is incredibly easy to let God in. When you were abusing yourself, God was there encouraging you to love yourself. When you were lying to others and treating others poorly, God was there encouraging you to love others. God has loved you from the beginning.

It is difficult to deny God because God lives inside of you. To deny God is to deny an essential part of yourself. We all know instinctively what is right and what is wrong. We do not have to be taught these things. The rules are the same across every culture and group. No matter where or how you were raised, the moral laws are the same and everyone knows them. We know not to lie or steal. We know to help others. We know to love ourselves.

Bad things happen because God allows free will. People hurt each other when they make choices independent of God's will. They can break God's law, and when this happens, there is great suffering. You probably have done some things that make you feel ashamed. You never would have felt this shame if you had followed God's plan.

"Where was God when I needed God?" many people cry. "Where was God when all those bad things were happening to me?" Well, the answer to those questions is that God was right there encouraging you to see the truth. God never promises that life is not going to hurt. God promises that he is there teaching you, educating you, and supporting you.

Do not be discouraged if you doubt God. Your doubt about God is not bad; it is good. It means that you think and reason. You should not blindly accept things without proof. That would be foolish. What you must know is this: Only God can overcome your doubt. There is nothing you can do to make doubt go away. You can only trust that if you seek God, then God will find you. Once God finds you, your doubt will be removed. Only by swimming in the sea of doubt can you learn how to swim with strong strokes. This is how your faith gets strong. No one is asking you to accept God blindly. Follow your AA/NA group. The group members know the way. Be willing to seek God. Open your heart and your mind in every way you know how. Seek the God of your understanding. Ask your clergy or your counselor for some reading. Go at your own rate.

Follow God in your own way. Soon you will find a peace that will surpass your understanding. This is the peace that we call serenity.

I am in the _____.

_____ Precontemplation stage

_____ Contemplation stage

_____ Preparation stage

_____ Action stage

_____ Maintenance stage

Step Three

[We] made a decision to turn our will and our lives over to the care of God as we understood Him.

—Alcoholics Anonymous (AA) (2001, p. 59)

Before beginning this exercise, please read Step Three in *Twelve Steps and Twelve Traditions* (AA, 2002).

You have come a long way in the program, and you can feel proud of yourself. You have decided that you are powerless over mood-altering chemicals and that your life is unmanageable. You have decided that a Higher Power of some sort can restore you to sanity. In Step Three, you will reach toward God—the God of your own understanding. You will consider using God as your Higher Power. This is the miracle. It is the major focus of the 12-step program. This is a spiritual program that directs you toward the ultimate truth. It is important that you be open to the possibility that there is a God. It is vital that you give this concept room to blossom and grow. The "Big Book" says, "That probably no human power could have relieved our alcoholism. That God could and would if He were sought" (AA, 2001, p. 60).

Step Three should not confuse you. It calls for a decision to correct your character defects under spiritual supervision. You must make an honest effort to change your life, and you are responsible for all of your choices. You have made some choices before that have hurt yourself and others. List 10 choices you made that hurt yourself or someone else.

1. _____

2. _____

3. _____

4. _____

5. _____

6. _____

7. _____

8. _____

9. _____

10. _____

Now it is time to make some different choices that will set you off on a new direction. Think about each choice carefully, and do not make a choice until you have carefully thought through the possible positive and negative consequences of your decision. The AA program is a spiritual program. About the Big Book, it states, "Its main object is to enable you to find a power greater than yourself that will solve your problem" (AA, 2001, p. 45). Both AA and Narcotics Anonymous (NA) clearly state that the God of your understanding is probably the answer to your problems. If you are willing to seek God, then you will find God. That is God's promise.

THE MORAL LAW

All spirituality has, at its core, what is already inside of you. You do not have to look very far for God. Your Higher Power lives inside of you. Inside of all of us, there is inherent goodness. In all cultures, and in all lands, this goodness is expressed in what we call the moral law. God has put his law inside of everyone's mind, body, and spirit. The law asks you to love yourself, others, and God in action and in truth. It is simply stated as follows: Love God all you can, love others all you can, and love yourself all you can. This law is very powerful. If some stranger were drowning in a pool next to you, then this internal law would motivate you to help. Instinctively, you would feel driven to help, even if it put your own life at risk. The moral law is so important that it transcends our instinct for survival. You would try to save that drowning person. This moral law is exactly the same everywhere and in every culture. It exists inside of everyone. It is written on your heart. Even among thieves, honesty is valued.

When we survey religious thought, we come up with many different ideas about God, but if we look at the saints of the religions, they are living practically indistinguishable lives. They all are doing the same things with their lives. They do not lie, cheat, or steal; they believe in giving to others before giving to themselves; they are humble; and they try not to be envious of what other people have. They are content with their life, grateful for everything they have, and good to themselves and others. To believe in your Higher Power, you must believe that this good exists inside of you. You also must believe that there is more of this goodness at work outside of you. If you do not believe in a living and breathing God at this point, do not worry. Every one of us has started where you are.

All people have a basic problem: We break the moral law, even if we believe in it.

This fact means that there is something wrong with us. We are incapable of following the moral law as we want to. Even though we would consider it unfair for someone to lie to us, occasionally we lie to someone else. If we see someone dressed in clothes that make the person look terrible, we might tell that person that he or she looks good.

This is a lie, and we would not want other people lying to us like that. In this and other situations, we do not obey the very moral law that we know is good.

You must ask yourself several questions. Where did we get this moral law? How did these laws of behavior get started? Did they just evolve over time or were they set by someone? If it was set by someone, how did this someone set the same laws in every heart in every part of the world? The program of AA/NA believes that these good laws come from something good and that there is more of this good at work in the universe. People in the program believe that people can communicate with this good, and they call this good *God*.

Do you believe that there is something good in the universe?

> Yes   No

Do you believe that there is something good inside of you?

> Yes   No

We do not know everything about the Higher Power. Much of God remains a mystery. If we look at science, we find the same thing: Most of science is a mystery. We know very little about the primary elements of science such as gravity or electromagnetic energy, but we can make judgments about these elements using our experience. No one has ever seen an electron, but we are sure that it exists because we have some experience of it. It is the same thing with the Higher Power. We can know that there is a power greater than we are if we have some experience of this power. Both science and spirituality necessitate a faith based on direct human experience.

There seems to emerge in people, as naturally as the ability to love, the ability to experience God. The experience cannot be taught. It is already there, and it must be awakened. It is primal, already planted, and awaiting growth. God is experienced as a force that is alive. This force is above and more capable than humans are. God is so good, pure, and perfect that God obeys the moral law all of the time. The experience of the Higher Power brings with it a feeling of great power and energy. This can be both attractive and frightening, but mainly you will find that God is loving. God has contacted humans through the ages and has said, "I am. I exist."

Do you believe that some sort of a Supreme Being exists?

> Yes   No

Instinctively, people know that if they can get more of this goodness then they will have better lives. Spirituality must be practical. It must make your life better or else you will discard it. If you open yourself up to the spiritual part of the program, then you will feel better immediately.

God knows that if you follow the law of love you will be happy. God makes love known to all people. It is born in everyone. The consequence for breaking the moral law is separation from God. This is experienced as deep emotional pain. We feel isolated, empty, frightened, and lonely.

Scripture tells us that God is hungry for your love. God desires a deep, personal relationship with you. All people have a similar instinctive hunger for God. By reading this exercise, you can begin to develop your relationship with God. You will find true joy here if you try. Without some sort of a Higher Power, your recovery will be more difficult. A Higher Power can relieve your addiction problem like nothing else can. Many people achieve stable recovery without calling their Higher Power *God*. That certainly is possible. There are many wonderful atheists and agnostics in our program, but the AA/NA way is to reach for some sort of a God of your own understanding.

You can change things in your life. You really can. You do not have to drown in despair any longer. No matter who you are, God loves you. God is willing to help you. Perhaps God has been waiting for you for a long time. Think of how wonderful it is. There is a God. God created you. God loves you. God has a purpose for your life, and God will show you the way. God wants you to be happy. Try to open yourself up to this experience.

THE KEY TO STEP THREE

The key to working Step Three is willingness—the willingness to turn your life over to the care of God as you understand him. This is difficult for many of us because we think that we are in control of everything and everyone. We are completely fooled by this delusion. We believe that we know the right thing to do. We believe that everything would be fine if others would just do things our way. This leads us to deep feelings of resentment and self-pity. People in our lives would not cooperate with all of our plans. No matter how hard we tried to control everything, things kept getting out of control. Sometimes the harder we worked, the nicer or meaner we acted, the worse things got.

You are not in control of the universe, and you never have been in control. Your Higher Power is in control. God is the only one who knows about everything. God created you and the universe. Chemically dependent persons, in many ways, are trying to be God. They want the universe to revolve around them. "Above everything, we alcoholics must be rid of this selfishness" (AA, 2001, p. 62).

HOW TO TURN IT OVER

To arrest addiction, you have to stop playing God and let your Higher Power take control. If you sincerely want this and you try, it is easy to do so. Go to a quiet place and talk to your Higher Power about your addiction. Say something like this:

- "God, I do not know if you are out there or not, but if you are, come into my life and help me. I cannot do this by myself anymore."
- Then ask God this question, "God, what is the next step in my relationship with you?"
- Wait and tune your mind, body, and spirit. Do not be afraid. Wait for one word or phrase to come into your mind. This will not be audible but an inaudible, tender thought. You might get words inside of your mind or see an image.

Write down exactly what came into your mind.

_____

_____

STEP THREE ■ 69

_____

_____

_____

This communication will be accompanied with a feeling of peace. The next time you have a problem, stop and turn the problem over to your Higher Power. Say something like this: "God, I cannot deal with this problem. You deal with it." Describe three times when this happened.

1. _____

2. _____

3. _____

As you ask for God's will to be done, you will find the right direction. God knows the way for you. If you follow your Higher Power, then you never will be lost again. God will encourage you to see the truth, and then God will leave the choices up to you. You always can decide. God wants you to be free. God wants you to make all of your own decisions, but God wants to have input into your decisions. Your Higher Power wants to show you the way. If you try to find the way by yourself, then you will ultimately slip off the path and find yourself lost. God promises that if you will follow God's plan then God will see to it that you receive all of the desires of your heart. God knows exactly what you need.

Step Three offers no compromise. It calls for a decision. Exactly how you surrender and turn things over is not the point. The important thing is that you are willing to try.

Can you see that it is necessary to give up your self-centeredness?

     Yes   No

Do you see that it is time to turn things over to a power greater than you are?

     Yes   No

List 10 things that you have to gain by turning your will and your life over to a Higher Power. Get your group or counselor to help you.

1. _____

2. _____

3. _____

4. _____

5. _____

6. _____

7. _____

8. _____

9. _____

10. _____

List five reasons why you need to turn things over to a power greater than yourself.

1. _____

2. _____

3. _____

4. _____

5. _____

We should not confuse organized religion with spirituality. In Step Two, you learned that spirituality deals with your relationship with yourself, others, and God. Religion is an organized system of faith and worship. It is person-made, not God-made. It is humans' way of interpreting God's plan. Religion can be confusing or helpful. It can even drive people away from God. Are old religious ideas keeping you away from trusting God? If so, then how?

A great barrier to your finding God may be impatience. You may want to find God right now. You must understand that your spiritual growth is set by God and not by you. You will grow spiritually when God knows you are ready. Remember that we are turning this whole thing over. Each person has his or her own unique spiritual journey. Each person must have his or her own individual walk. Spiritual growth, not perfection, is your goal. All you can do is seek the God of your understanding. When God knows that you are ready, God will find you. Finally, you will want to surrender to God's will for your life. If you are holding back, then you need to let go absolutely. Faith, willingness, and prayer will overcome all of the obstacles. Do not worry about your doubt. Just keep seeking in every way you know how.

List 10 ways in which you can seek God. Ask your friends or counselor to help you.

1. _____

2. _____

3. _____

4. _____

5. _____

6. _____

7. _____

8. _____

9. _____

10. _____

What does the AA saying "Let go and let God" mean to you?

_____

_____

_____

_____

_____

List five ways in which you can put Step Three to work in your life.

1. _____

2. _____

3. _____

4. _____

5. _____

List the things in your life you still want to control.

_____

_____

_____

_____

_____

How can these things be handled better by turning them over to your Higher Power?

_____

_____

_____

_____

_____

List five ways in which you allowed chemicals to be the God in your life.

1. _____

2. _____

3. _____

4. _____

5. _____

List three ways your chemical use separated you from God.

1. _____

2. _____

3. _____

What changes have you noticed in yourself since you entered the program?

_____

_____

_____

_____

Of these changes, which of them occurred because you listened to someone else other than yourself?

_____

_____

_____

_____

Make a list of the things that are holding you back from turning things over.

1. _____

2. _____

3. _____

4. _____

5. _____

List five ways you see God taking care of you.

1. _____

2. _____

3. _____

4. _____

5. _____

How do you understand God now?

_____

_____

_____

_____

_____

_____

HOW TO PRAY

Pray by reading the Step Three prayer once each day for a week. Say the words carefully aloud, and listen to yourself as you speak. Feel God's presence with you, and when you are ready, begin to talk to God. Make prayer a dialogue, not a monologue. Talk to God, and then listen for God's answer to come to you inside of your mind.

God I offer myself to Thee—to build with me and to do with me as Thou wilt. Relieve me of the bondage of self, that I may better do Thy will. Take away my difficulties, that victory over them may bear witness to those I would help of Thy Power, Thy Love, and Thy Way of Life. May I do Thy will always! (AA, 2001, p. 63)

Listen for God in others. God may speak to you through them. Look for God's actions in the group, in the weather, and in nature. Read Scripture, and seek God through your reading. Ask your counselor or your clergyperson for some suggestions.

HOW TO MEDITATE

Take time to meditate each day. Sit in a quiet place for about 10 to 20 minutes, and pay attention to your breathing. Ask God this question: "God, what do you have to say to me today?" Then empty your mind. Do not be nervous if there is only silence for a while. Listen for God's message for you. Write down any words or images that come into your mind. Keep a log of each meditation for a week.

Day 1. _____

Day 2. _____

Day 3. _____

Day 4. _____

Day 5. _____

Day 6. _____

Day 7. _____

Make a list of what are you going to do on a daily basis to help your spiritual program grow.

_____

_____

_____

_____

_____

Trust that if you seek God, then God will find you—no matter who you are, no matter where you are. God loves you more than you can imagine. You are God's perfect child, created in God's image. God has great plans for you.

I am in the _____.

_____ Precontemplation stage

_____ Contemplation stage

_____ Preparation stage

_____ Action stage

_____ Maintenance stage

Step Four

[We] made a searching and fearless moral inventory of ourselves.

—Alcoholics Anonymous (AA) (2001, p. 59)

Before beginning this exercise, please read Step Four in *Twelve Steps and Twelve Traditions* (AA, 2002).

Congratulations! You are doing well in the program. You have admitted your power-lessness over alcohol or drugs, and you have found a Higher Power that can restore you to sanity. Now you must up your maladaptive thoughts and behavior by taking a careful inventory of yourself. You must know exactly what resources you have available, and you must examine the exact nature of your wrongs. You need to be detailed about the good things about your choices and the bad choices you have made. Only by taking this inventory will you know exactly where you are. Then you can decide where you are going.

In taking this inventory, you must be detailed and specific. It is the only way of see-ing the complete impact of your disease. A part of the truth might be, "I told lies to my children." The complete truth might be, "I told my children that I had cancer. They were terrified and cried for a long time." These two statements would be very different. Only the second statement tells the exact nature of the wrong, and the client felt the full impact of the disclosure. You can see how important it is to put the whole truth before you at one time.

Remember, the truth will set you free from the slavery to the addiction.

The Fourth Step is a long autobiography of your life. Read this exercise before you start, and underline things that pertain to you. You will want to come back and cover each of these issues in detail as you write your whole story down. If the problem does not relate to you, then leave it blank. Examine exactly what you did wrong. Look for your mistakes even though the situation was not totally your fault. Try to disregard what the other person did and to concentrate on what you did. It is also important to write down what you were thinking that led to your bad choices. In time, you will realize that the person who hurt you was as spiritually sick as you were. You need to ask your Higher Power to help you forgive that person or to show that person the same forgive-ness that you would want for yourself. You can honestly pray that the other person finds out the truth about what he or she did to you.

Review your natural desires carefully and think about how you acted on them. You will see that some of them became the Higher Powers of your life. Sex, food, money, relation-ships, power, influence, education, and many others can become the major focus of your life. The pursuit of these desires can take total control and can become the center of our existence. That is when we insult God. We say that these objects can make us happy and save us. Making good choices sets us free from the old behavior of the past. Once we begin to think, feel, and act accurately, we enjoy the positive consequences of our actions. If we continue to think inaccurately, we will feel and act in a way that hurts others and ourselves. We can always stop, think, and plan before we act. It helps to role-play difficulties we have had in the past in skills group so we can learn new ways of thinking and acting. Many of us have one feeling that leads to one action. The truth is we can stop when we feel, get our thoughts and feelings accurate, and then find many ways we can cope with the situation.

In working through the Fourth Step inventory, you will experience pain. You will feel angry, sad, fearful, ashamed, embarrassed, guilty, and lonely. The Fourth Step is a grieving process. As you see clearly your inaccurate, thoughts, feelings, and behaviors, you may feel that no one will ever love you again, but remember that God created you in perfection. You are God's perfect child, God's masterpiece, God's work of art. There is nothing wrong with you. You have everything that you need to be happy, joyous, and free. Sure, you made some mistakes. That is an essential part of life. We learn from our mistakes. Once you clean house, you can begin to purify yourself by shedding your defects of character. These are our old sick ways of thinking, feeling, and acting. These character defects will not go away easily, and you will feel the old behaviors fight for life. You have grown comfortable in the lies, and now you are walking into the truth. You are walking out of the darkness and into the light—out of the fear and into the peace that AA calls serenity.

Now let us take a basic look at right and wrong. We cover the following areas.

1. Did God come first in your life? Did you seek and follow God's will at all times?

   a. List your idols—money, fame, position, alcohol, drugs, sex, power, relationships?

   b. Have you always honored God with your language? List three ways you dishonored God with your actions or words.

      (1) _____

      (2) _____

      (3) _____

   c. Have you always set aside a day to improve your relationship with God?

   d. Have you loved, honored, and respected your parents? List at least five ways you dishonored your mother and father.

      (1) _____

      (2) _____

      (3) _____

(4) _____

(5) _____

   e. Make a list of your unresolved hate, anger, and resentments.

   f. List your adulterous acts or thoughts.

   g. List when you cheated, misrepresented yourself, made pressure deals, or had bad debts.

   h. List the times you slandered another person or spread gossip.

   i. List the times you lusted after something that belonged to someone else or felt envious or overly competitive.

2. Take a close look at any false pride.

   a. Egotistical vanity is having too great an admiration of yourself. Pride makes you your own law, moral judge, and Higher Power.

     (1) List three times you boasted or self-glorified yourself with lies.

       1. _____

       2. _____

       3. _____

     (2) Discuss your love of publicity.

     (3) List five times you lied to pretend to be better than others are.

       1. _____

       2. _____

       3. _____

       4. _____

       5. _____

     (4) List three times you refused to give up your will.

       1. _____

       2. _____

       3. _____

(5) List at least three times you resented someone who you thought crossed you.

1. _____

2. _____

3. _____

(6) List three times when you quarreled when another person challenged your wishes.

1. _____

2. _____

3. _____

(7) List five times when you knew you were disobeying or refusing to submit your will to the will of your superiors or to God.

1. _____

2. _____

3. _____

4. _____

5. _____

3. Take a close look at any greed.

Do you desire wealth, such as money or other things, as an end in itself rather than as a means to an end? In acquiring wealth in any form, do you disregard the rights of others? Do you give an honest day's work for an honest day's pay? How do you use what you have? Are you stingy with your friends and family? Do you love money and possessions for these things in themselves? How excessive is your love of luxury? Do you stoop to devices such as fraud, perjury, dishonesty, and sharp practices in dealing with others? Do you try to fool yourself in these regards? Do you call questionable business "Big Business"? Do you call unreasonable hoarding "security"? Will you do almost anything to attain these things and kid yourself by giving your methods innocent names?

4. Take a close look at any lust.

Lust is inordinate love and desire of the pleasures of the flesh. Are you guilty of lust in any of its forms? Do you tell yourself that improper or undue indulgence in sexual activities is okay? Do you treat people as objects of your desire other than as God's perfect creations? Do you use pornography or think unhealthy sexual thoughts? Do you treat other people sexually the same way in which you would want to be treated? Do you love others the same way in which you want them to love you?

5. Take a close look at any envy.

   Do you dislike seeing others happy or successful, as though they had stolen something from you? Do you resent those who are smarter than you are? Do you criticize the good done by others because you secretly wish that you had done it yourself? Are you ever envious enough to try to lower another person's reputation by starting or engaging in gossip about that person? Do you call religious people "hypocrites" because they go to church and try to be religiously good even though they are subject to human failings? Do you ever accuse the educated, wise, or learned of being highbrow because you envy their advantages? Do you genuinely love other people, or do you find them distasteful because you envy them?

6. Take a close look at any anger.

   Do you ever fly into a rage of temper, become revengeful, or entertain urges to "get even" or an "I would not let him get away with it" attitude? Do you ever resort to violence, clench your fists, or stomp about in a temper flare-up? Are you touchy, unduly sensitive, or impatient at the smallest thing? Do you ever murmur or grumble even in small matters? Do you ignore the fact that anger prevents development of personality and halts spiritual progress? Do you realize that anger often ruins good judgment? Do you permit anger to rule you when you know that it blinds you to the rights of others? Do you permit yourself to become angry when others are weak and become angry with you? Do you find yourself in a rage when someone criticizes you even for small things?

7. Take a close look at any overindulgence.

   Do you weaken your moral and intellectual life by excessive use of food and drink? Do you generally eat to excess and, thus, enslave your soul and character to the pleasures of the body beyond the reasonable needs of the body? Did you ever, when drinking or using drugs, become nauseated and vomit, only to immediately return and drink or use some more? Did you use so much that your intellect and personality deteriorated? So much that memory, judgment, and concentration were affected? So much that personal pride and social judgment vanished? So much that you developed a spirit of despair?

8. Take a look at any laziness.

   Are you finding yourself being lazy or given to idleness, procrastination, nonchalance, and indifference in material things? Are you lukewarm in prayer? Do you hold the self-discipline of others in contempt? Are you fainthearted in performance of those things that are morally or spiritually difficult? Are you ever listless with aversion to effort in any form? Are you easily distracted from things spiritual, quickly turning to things temporal?

PERSONALITY DEFECTS

1. Selfishness

   This is taking care of one's own needs without regard for others.

   a. Example: The family would like to go on an outing. Dad would like drinking, golfing, or fishing, or he has a hangover. Who wins?

   b. Example: Your child needs a new pair of shoes. You put it off until payday but get a fifth that same night.

   c. You are afraid to dance because you might appear awkward.

2. Alibis

   This is the highly developed art of justifying our chemical use and behavior through excuses such as the following:

   a. "A few will straighten me out."

   b. "Starting tomorrow, I am going to change."

   c. "If I did not have a wife and family . . ."

   d. "If I could start all over again . . ."

   e. "A drink will help me think."

   f. "Nobody cares anyway."

   g. "I had a hard day."

3. Dishonest thinking

   We take truths or facts and twist them to come up with the conclusions we need such as the following examples:

   a. "My secret love is going to raise the roof if I drop her. It is not fair to burden my wife with that sort of knowledge. Therefore, I will hang on to my girlfriend. This mess is not her fault."

   b. "If I tell my family about the $500 bonus, it will all go for bills. I have got to have some drinking money. Why start a family argument? I would leave well enough alone."

   c. "My spouse dresses well and eats well, and the kids are getting a good education. What more do they want from me?"

4. Shame

   This is the feeling that something irreparable is wrong with us.

   a. No matter how many people tell you that it is okay, you continue to berate yourself. List the things you cannot forgive yourself for doing.

   b. You keep going over and over your mistakes, wallowing in what a terrible person you are.

5. Resentment

   a. This is displeasure aroused by a real or imagined wrong or injury accompanied by irritation.

      (1) You are fired from work. You hate the boss.

      (2) Your sister warns you about excessive drinking. You get fighting mad at her.

(3) A coworker is doing a good job and gets accolades. You have a drug record and fear that this coworker might have been promoted over you. You hate his guts.

(4) You may have resentment toward a person or a group of people, or you may resent an institution, a religion, and so on.

b. Anger and resentment lead to bickering, friction, hatred, and unjust revenge. It brings out the worst in our immaturity and produces misery for ourselves and all concerned.

6. Intolerance

This is the refusal to put up with beliefs, practices, customs, or habits that differ from our own.

a. Do you hate other people because they are of another race, come from a different country, or have a different religion?

b. Did you have any choice in being born a particular color or nationality?

c. Isn't our religion usually "inherited"?

7. Impatience

This is an unwillingness to calmly bear delay, opposition, pain, or bother.

a. A chemically dependent person is someone who jumps on a horse and gallops off madly in all directions at the same time.

b. Do you blow your stack when someone keeps you waiting over the "allotted time" you gave that person?

c. Did anyone ever have to wait for you?

8. Phoniness

This is a manifestation of our false pride or the old false front.

a. I present my love with a present as evidence of my love. Just by pure coincidence, it helps to smooth over my last binge.

b. I buy new clothes because my business position demands it. Meanwhile, the family also could use food and clothes.

9. Procrastination

This is putting off or postponing things that need to be done—the familiar "I would do it tomorrow."

a. Did little jobs that were put off become big and almost impossible later?

b. Do you pamper yourself by doing things "my way"?

c. Can you handle little jobs that you are asked to take care of, or do you feel picked on?

d. Little things, done for God, make them great. Are you doing the little things for God?

10. Self-pity

a. These people at the party are having fun with their drinking. Why can't I be like that? This is the "woe is me" syndrome.

b. If I had that person's money, then I would not have any problems. This is a similar attitude.

11. Feelings too easily hurt

   a. I walk down the street and say hello to someone. The person does not answer. I am hurt and furious.

   b. I am expecting my turn at the AA meeting, but the time runs out. I feel rejected.

12. Fear

   This is an inner foreboding, whether real or imagined, of doom ahead. We suspect that our use of chemicals, behavior, negligence, and so on are catching up with us. We fear the worst.

   When we learn to accept our powerlessness, ask our Higher Power for help, and face ourselves with honesty, the nightmare will be gone.

13. Depression

   This is feeling sad or down most of the day.

   a. You keep going over all of the things that are going wrong.

   b. You tend to think the worst.

14. Feelings of inadequacy

   This is feeling as though you cannot do it.

   You hold on to a negative self-image even when you succeed.

15. Perfectionism

   You have to do everything perfect all of the time.

   a. Even when you have done a good job, you find something wrong with it.

   b. Someone compliments you on something. You feel terrible because it could have been better.

PHYSICAL LIABILITIES

1. Diseases, disabilities, and other physical limitations about how you look or how your body functions

2. Sexual problems or hang-ups

3. Negative feelings about your appearance

4. Negative feelings about your age

5. Negative feelings about your sex

TIME-OUT

If you have gone through the exercise to this point without coming up for air—it figures. We did our drinking and drugging the same way. Whoa! Easy does it! Take this in reasonable stages. Assimilate each portion of the exercise thoughtfully. The reading of this is important, but the application of it is even more important. Take some time to think and rest, and let it settle in. Develop some sort of a workable daily plan. Include plenty of rest.

When chemically dependent people stop using, part of their lives is taken away from them. This is a terrible loss to sustain unless it is replaced by something else. We cannot just boot the chemicals out the window. They meant too much to us. They were how we faced life, the key to escape, and the tool for solving life's problems. In approaching a new way of life, a new set of tools is substituted. These are the 12 steps and the AA/Narcotics Anonymous (NA) way of life.

The same principle applies when we eliminate our character defects. We replace them by substituting assets that are better adapted to a healthy lifestyle. As with substance use, you do not fight a defect. You replace it with something that works better. Use what follows for further character analysis and as a guide for character building. These are the new tools. The objective is not perfection but rather progress. You will be happy with the type of living that produces self-respect, respect and love for others, and security from the nightmare of addiction.

THE WAY TO RECOVERY

1. Faith

   This is the act of leaving that part of our lives to the care of a power greater than ourselves with assurance that it will work out. This will be shaky at first, but with it comes a deep spiritual connection.

   a. Faith is acquired through application—acceptance, daily prayer, and meditation.

   b. We depend on faith. We have faith that the lights will come on, that the car will start, and that our coworkers will handle their end of things.

   c. Spiritual faith is the acceptance of our gifts, limitations, problems, and trials with equal gratitude, knowing that God has a plan for us. With "Thy will be done" as our daily guide, we will lose our fear and find ourselves.

2. Hope

   Faith suggests reliance. We came to believe that a power greater than ourselves would restore us to sanity. We hope to stay clean and sober, regain our self-respect, and love our families. Hope resolves itself into a driving force. It gives purpose to our daily living.

   a. Faith gives us direction, and hope gives us the steam to take action.

   b. Hope reflects a positive attitude. Things are going to work out for us if we work the program.

3. Love

   This is the active involvement in someone's individual growth.

   a. Love must occur in action and in truth.

   b. "Love is patient, love is kind."

   c. In its deeper sense, love is the art of living realistically and fully, guided by spiritual awareness of our responsibilities and our debt of gratitude to God and to others.

Analysis. Have you used the qualities of faith, hope, and love in your past? How will they apply to your new way of life?

WE STAY ON TRACK THROUGH ACTION

1. *Courtesy:* Some of us are actually afraid to be gentle persons.

2. *Cheerfulness:* Circumstances do not determine our frame of mind. We do. "Today I will be cheerful. I will look for the beauty in life."

3. *Order:* Live today only. Organize one day at a time.

4. *Loyalty:* Be faithful to whom you believe in.

5. *Use of time:* Use your time wisely.

6. *Punctuality:* This includes self-discipline, order, and consideration for others.

7. *Sincerity:* This is the mark of self-respect and genuineness. Sincerity carries conviction and generates enthusiasm. It is contagious.

8. *Caution in speech:* Watch your tongue. We can be vicious and thoughtless. Too often, the damage is irreparable.

9. *Kindness:* This is one of life's great satisfactions. We do not have real happiness until we have given of ourselves. Practice this daily.

10. *Patience:* This is the antidote to resentments, self-pity, and impulsiveness.

11. *Tolerance:* This requires common courtesy, courage, and a "live and let live" attitude.

12. *Integrity:* This includes the ultimate qualifications of a person—honesty, loyalty, and sincerity.

13. *Balance:* Do not take yourself too seriously. We get a better perspective when we can laugh at ourselves.

14. *Gratitude:* The person without gratitude is filled with false pride. Gratitude is the honest recognition of help received. Use it often.

Analysis. In considering the little virtues, where did I fail, and how did that contribute to my accumulated problem? What virtues should I pay attention to in this rebuilding program?

PHYSICAL ASSETS

1. *Physical Health:* How healthy am I despite any ailments?

_____

_____

_____

_____

_____

2. *Talents:* What am I good at?

_____

_____

_____

_____

3. *Age:* At my age, what can I offer to others?

_____

_____

_____

_____

4. *Sexuality:* How can I use my sexuality to express my love?

_____

_____

_____

_____

5. *Knowledge:* How can I use my knowledge and experience to help myself and others?

_____

_____

_____

_____

_____

MENTAL ASSETS

1. Despite your problems, how healthy are you emotionally?

2. Do you care for others? Make a list of the ways you can share your experience, strength, and hope.

3. Are you kind?

4. Can you be patient? List some ways you can give others the time to think, plan, and act.

5. Are you basically a good person? In detail, describe the person you want to be.

6. Do you want to help others? List five ways you can help other people.

    1. _____

    2. _____

    3. _____

    4. _____

    5. _____

7. Do you try to tell the truth?

8. Do you try to be forgiving? List the people you are still having trouble forgiving, and turn them over to God.

9. Can you be enthusiastic?

10. Are you sensitive to the needs of others?

11. Can you be serene? Make plans to meditate every day by reading AA/NA material, Scripture, or other recovery reading.

12. *Sincerity:* How are you going to try to be sincere?

13. *Self-discipline:* List the ways you are going to try to bring order and self-control into your life.

14. Are you going to accept the responsibility for your own behavior and stop blaming others?

15. How are you going to use your intelligence?

16. Are you going to seek the will of God?

17. *Education:* How might you improve your mind in furthering your education?

18. Are you going to be grateful for what you have?

19. *Integrity:* How can you improve your honesty and reliability?

20. *Joy:* In what areas of your life do you find happiness?

21. Are you humble and working on your false pride?

22. Are you seeking the Higher Power of your own understanding?

23. *Acceptance:* In what ways can you better accept your own limitations and the limitations of others?

24. *Courage:* Are you willing to trust and follow the God of your understanding?

THE AUTOBIOGRAPHY

Using this exercise, write the story of your life. Cover your experiences in 5-year intervals. Be brief, but try not to miss anything. Tell the whole truth. Write down exactly what you thought and did. Consider all of the things that you marked during the exercise. Read the exercise again if you need to do so. Make an exhaustive and honest consideration of your past and present. Cover both assets and liabilities carefully. You will rebuild your life on the solid building blocks of your assets. These are the tools of recovery. Omit nothing because of shame, embarrassment, or fear. Determine the thoughts, feelings, and actions that plagued you. You want to meet these problems face-to-face and see them in writing. If you wish, you may destroy your inventory after completing the Fifth Step. Many clients hold a ceremony in which they burn the Fourth Step inventory. This symbolizes that they are leaving the old life behind. They are starting a new life free of the past.

I am in the _____.

_____ Precontemplation stage

_____ Contemplation stage

_____ Preparation stage

_____ Action stage

_____ Maintenance stage

Step Five

[We] admitted to God, ourselves, and to another human being the exact nature of our wrongs.

—Alcoholics Anonymous (2001, p. 57)

Before beginning this exercise, please read Step Five in *Twelve Steps and Twelve Traditions* (AA, 2002).

With Steps One through Four behind you, it is now time to clean house and start over. You must free yourself of the guilt and shame and go forward in a new life full of faith and hope. The Fifth Step is meant to right the wrongs with your Higher Power, yourself, and others. You will develop a new attitude and a new relationship, particularly with yourself. You have admitted your powerlessness, and you have identified your liabilities and assets in the personal inventory. Now it is time to get right with your Higher Power. You will do this by admitting to God, to yourself, and to another person the exact nature of your wrongs. You are going to cover all of your assets and liabilities in the Fifth Step. You are going to tell someone the whole truth at one time. This person is important because he or she is a symbol of God and everyone else. You must watch this person's face. The illness has been telling you that if you tell anyone the whole truth about you, people will not like you. That is a lie, and you are going to prove that it is a lie. The truth is this: Unless you tell people the truth, they cannot like you, because they do not know you. You must see yourself tell someone the truth and watch that person's reaction.

It is very difficult to discuss your faults with someone. It is hard enough just thinking about them yourself, but this is a necessary step. It will help to free you from the shame and guilt of the addictive behavior. You must tell this person everything, the whole story, all of the things that you are afraid to share. If you withhold anything, then you will not get the relief you need to start over. You will be carrying around excess baggage. You do not need to do this to yourself. God loves you and wants you to be free of guilt, shame, and hurt. God wants you to be happy and to reach your full potential.

Time after time, newcomers have tried to keep to themselves certain facts about their lives. Trying to avoid this humbling experience, they have turned to easier methods. Almost invariably, they got drunk. Having persevered with the rest of the program, they wondered why they fell. We think the reason is that they never completed their housecleaning. They took inventory all right but hung on to some of the worst items in stock. They only *thought* they had lost their egotism and fear;

they only *thought* they had humbled themselves. But they had not learned enough of humility, fearlessness, and honesty, in the sense we find necessary, until they told someone else *all* their life story. (AA, 2001, pp. 72–73)

By finally telling someone the whole truth, you will rid yourself of that terrible sense of isolation and loneliness. You will feel a new sense of belonging, acceptance, and freedom. If you do not immediately feel relief, do not worry. If you have been completely honest, then the relief will come. "The dammed-up emotions of years break out of their confinement and miraculously vanish when they are exposed" (AA, 2001, p. 62). You can be forgiven, no matter what you have done. You are God's child, and he wants to make you into a new person who is dedicated to helping others.

The Fifth Step will develop within you a new humbleness of character that is necessary for normal living. You will come to recognize who and what you are. When you are honest with another person, it confirms that you have been honest with yourself and with God.

The person with whom you will share your Fifth Step has been chosen carefully for you. You will meet with this person several times before you do the step. You need to decide whether you can trust this person. Do you believe that this person is confidential? Do you feel comfortable with this person? Do you believe that this person will understand?

Once you have chosen that person, put your false pride aside and go for it. Tell this person everything about yourself. Do not leave one dark act untold. Tell this person about all of the good things as well as all of the bad things you have done. Share the details, and do not leave anything out. If it troubles you even a little, then share it. Let it all hang out to be examined by God, by you, and by that other person. Every good and bad part needs to be revealed. When you are finished, say a prayer to your Higher Power. Tell God that you are sorry for what you have done wrong, and commit yourself to a new way of life following the God of your understanding. Many clients like to say the Seventh Step prayer:

My Creator, I am now willing that you should have all of me, good and bad. I pray that you now remove from me every single defect of character, which stands in the way of my usefulness to you and my fellows. Grant me strength, as I go out from here, to do your bidding. (AA, 2001, p. 76)

I am in the _____.

_____ Precontemplation stage

_____ Contemplation stage

_____ Preparation stage

_____ Action stage

_____ Maintenance stage

Stress Management

Unresolved stress fuels addiction. Addicted individuals deal with stress by using chemicals or addictive behavior rather than using other more appropriate coping skills. Everyone has stress, and everyone needs to learn how to cope with stress in daily life. Stress is the generalized physiological response to a stressor. A stressor is any demand made on the body.

A stressor can be anything that mobilizes the body for change. This can include psychological or physiological loss, absence of stimulation, excessive stimulation, frustration of an anticipated reward, conflict, and presentation or anticipation of painful events (Zegans, 1982).

The stress response is good and adaptive. It activates the body for problem solving. Stress is destructive only when it is chronic. The overly stressed body produces harmful chemicals such as cortisol that triggers inflammation, and soon the person gets sick. Initially, the body produces certain chemicals to handle the stressful situation. Initially, these chemical changes are adaptive. In the end, they are destructive. Severe or chronic stress has been linked to irreversible disease including kidney impairment, hypertension, arteriosclerosis, type 2 diabetes, ulcers, and a compromised immune system that can result in increased infections and cancer (Selye, 1956).

When animals encounter an unsolvable problem, they ultimately get sick. They fall victim to a wide variety of physical and mental disorders. Under chronic stress, these organisms ultimately die.

It seems that everyone has a genetic predisposition to break down in a certain organ system when under chronic stress. Some people get depressed; some have ulcers, heart attacks, strokes, and some become chemically dependent.

In treatment, you must learn how to deal with stress in ways other than by using your addiction. You must learn to use the stress signals that your body gives you to help you solve problems. If you cannot solve the problem yourself, then you need to get some help.

Most people who are addicted are dealing with unresolved pain. They begin drinking, gambling, or using chemicals to ease the pain, and soon they become dependent. Addiction is a primary disease. It takes over people's lives and makes everything worse.

Stress management techniques help addicted individuals to regain the control they have lost in their lives. By establishing and maintaining a daily program of recovery, they learn how to cope with stress. If you are dealing with stress better, then you are not as likely to relapse. There are three elements necessary to reduce your overall stress level: (1) a regular exercise program, (2) regular relaxation, and (3) creating a more rewarding lifestyle.

RELAXATION

For centuries, people have relaxed or used meditation to quiet their minds and reach a state of peace. When animals have enough to eat and they are safe, they lay down. People do not do that because humans are the only animals that worry about the future. Humans fear that if they relax today, then they will be in trouble tomorrow.

Benson (1975, 2000) showed that when people relax twice a day for 10 to 20 minutes, it has a major impact on their overall stress levels. People who do this have fewer illnesses, feel better, and are healthier. Illness such as high blood pressure, ulcers, and headaches can go away completely with a regular relaxation program.

Benson maintained that the relaxation technique is simple.

1. Sit or lie down in a quiet place.

2. Pay attention to your breathing.

3. Every time you exhale, say the word *one* over quietly to yourself. It is normal for other ideas to come, but when they do, just return to the word or words you have chosen.

4. Do this for 10 to 20 minutes twice a day.

You do not have to use the word *one*. You can use any other word or phrase of your choice, but it has to be the same word or phrase over and over again. You can get some relaxation tapes or music that you find relaxing. You can pray or meditate. The most important thing is to relax as completely as you can. If you do this, then your stress level will be lower and you will be better able to mobilize yourself to deal with

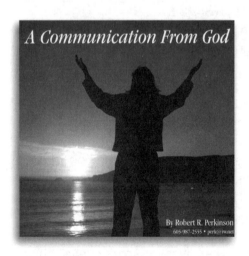

stress when it occurs. I have created a meditation exercise CD that you might find helpful. You can find this at www.cdbaby.com/cd/godtalks2. This tape has two tracks. Track 1 is a 20-minute spiritual exercise followed by relaxing music. Track 2 is a 12-minute meditation exercise followed by relaxing music. Many of our clients find this to be the turning point in their spiritual connection because it is the first time they experience the presence of God.

Progressive relaxation is tightening each muscle group and then relaxing them. For example, you tighten your right arm and feel the tension. Then let the muscle go and feel it deeply relax. Concentrate on the feeling of tension and relaxation. Soon you will not have to tighten the muscle group as often; you will just have to concentrate on it relaxing. As you practice relaxation, you will learn how it feels to be relaxed. Try to keep this feeling all day long.

- When you feel stressed, stop and take two deep breaths.
- Breathe in through your nose and out through your mouth.
- As you exhale, feel a warm wave of relaxation flow down your body.

- Once you have regained your state of relaxation, return to your day and move a little slower this time.
- Remember, nothing is ever done too well or too slowly. You do not have to do things quickly to succeed.

When you come to some new task that you think you have to complete, ask yourself several important questions.

1. Do I have to do this?

2. Do I have to do it now?

3. Is this going to make a difference in 5 years?

If the new stressor is not that important, perhaps you should not do it at all. Do not overly stress yourself. That does not make any sense. Know your limits. Achieve a state of relaxation in the morning, and listen to your body all day long. If anything threatens your serenity, turn it over and let God deal with it.

For the next week, set aside two times a day for relaxation. Go through the meditation exercise we discussed or some other relaxation exercise. Score the level of relaxation you achieved from 1 (*as little as possible*) to 100 (*as much as possible*). Then score your general stress level during the day in the same way. Write down any comments about your stress. List the situations when you felt the most tension.

Day 1

Relaxation Score

Daily Stress Score

Comments

Day 2

Relaxation Score

Daily Stress Score

Comments

Day 3

Relaxation Score

Daily Stress Score

Comments

Day 4

Relaxation Score

Daily Stress Score

Comments

Day 5

Relaxation Score

Daily Stress Score

Comments

Day 6

Relaxation Score

Daily Stress Score

Comments

Day 7

Relaxation Score

Daily Stress Score

Comments

EXERCISE

The role of exercise in the treatment of addiction has been well established. Significant improvements in physical fitness can occur in as short a period as 20 days. People who maintain a regular exercise program feel less depressed and less anxious, improve their self-concepts, and enhance the quality of their lives (Folkins & Sime, 1981).

Most addicted people come into treatment in poor physical and mental shape. They gave up on exercise a long time ago. Even if they were in good physical condition at one time in their lives, the addiction has taken its toll. These people are unable to maintain a consistent level of physical fitness. The mind and body cannot maintain a regular exercise program when a person chronically abuses drugs, alcohol, or other addictive behaviors.

An exercise program, although difficult to develop, can be fun. You get a natural high from exercise that you do not get in any other way. It feels good, and it feels good all day.

A good exercise program includes three elements: (1) stretching, (2) strength, and (3) cardiovascular fitness. The recreational therapist or personal trainer will assist you in developing an individualized program specific to you.

Stretching means that you increase a muscle's range of motion until you become supple and flexible. Never stretch your muscles to the point of pain. The body will warn you well before you go too far. Let the exercise therapist show you how to stretch each major muscle group. Get into a habit of stretching before all exercise.

In a strength program, you gradually lift more weight until you become stronger. Do not lift more often than every other day. The muscles need a full day of rest to repair them. Soon you can increase the load. Three sets of 8 to 12 repetitions each is a standard exercise for each muscle group. The exercise therapist will show you how to complete each exercise. Correct technique is very important.

Endurance training means that you exercise at a training heart rate for an extended period of time. This is where the cardiovascular system gets stronger. Your training heart rate is calculated by taking your age, minus the number 220, multiplied by .75.

Cardiovascular fitness is attained when you exercise at a training heart rate, for 20 to 30 minutes, at least three times a week. Have the exercise therapist help you to determine your training heart rate and develop a program in which you gradually increase your cardiovascular fitness. Usually, you will be increasing your exercise by 10% each week.

Many forms of exercise can be beneficial for cardiovascular training. The key point is this: It must be sustained exercise for at least 20 to 30 minutes. Walking is probably the best exercise to start with. It is easy to do, and you do not need any specialized equipment. The exercise cannot be a stop–start exercise such as tennis or golf. It must be something that you can sustain. These include exercises such as walking, jogging, swimming, and biking.

After you have worked out your exercise program, keep a daily log of your exercise. Reinforce yourself when you reach one of your goals. You might have a goal of running a mile by the end of the month. If you reach your goal, then buy yourself something you want or treat yourself to a movie to celebrate. Write down your exercise schedule for the next month.

EXERCISE PROGRAM

Date   *Training Heart Rate*

Strength

Stretching

Cardiovascular fitness

CHANGING YOUR LIFESTYLE

Along with maintaining a regular relaxation and exercise time, you must change other aspects of your life to improve your stress management skills.

Problem Solving Skills

You need to be able to identify and respond to the problems in your life. Unsolved problems increase your stress level. Problems are a normal part of life, and you need specific skills to deal with them effectively. For each problem that you encounter, work through the following steps:

1. Identify the problem.

2. Clarify your goals. What do you want?

3. Consider all the alternatives of action.

4. Think through each alternative, eliminating one at a time, until you have the best alternative.

5. Act on the problem.

6. Evaluate the effect of your action.

Work through several problems with your counselor or group while in treatment. See how effective it is to seek the advice and counsel of others. You need to ask for help.

Developing Pleasurable Activities

One of the things that chemically dependent people fear the most is not being able to have fun when clean and sober. Chemicals have been involved in pleasurable activities for so long that they are directly equated with all pleasure. To look forward to a life without being able to have fun is intolerable.

You do not give up fun in sobriety. You change the way in which you have fun. You cannot use chemicals for pleasure anymore. This is not good for you. You can enjoy many pleasant activities without drugs or alcohol. If you think about it, this is real fun anyway. The fun you are missing is based on a false chemically created feeling. Once you see how much fun you can have when clean and sober, you will be amazed.

Increasing pleasurable activities will elevate your mood and decrease your overall stress level. If you are not feeling well in recovery, it is likely that you are not involved in enough pleasurable activities. If you increase the level of pleasure, then you will feel better and be less vulnerable to relapse.

First, identify the things that you might enjoy doing, and then make a list of the things that you are going to do more often. Make a list of the activities that you plan to do for yourself each day. Write down your plan. The more pleasurable things you do, the better you will feel.

1. Being in the country

2. Wearing expensive clothes

3. Talking about sports

4. Meeting someone new

5. Going to a concert

6. Playing baseball or softball

7. Planning trips or vacations

8. Buying things for yourself

9. Going to the beach

10. Doing artwork

11. Rock climbing or mountaineering

12. Playing golf

13. Reading

14. Rearranging or redecorating your room or house

15. Playing basketball or volleyball

16. Going to a lecture

17. Breathing the clean air

18. Writing a song

19. Boating

20. Pleasing your parents

21. Watching television

22. Thinking quietly

23. Camping

24. Working on machines (e.g., cars, bikes, motors)

25. Working in politics

26. Thinking about something good in the future

27. Playing cards

28. Laughing

29. Working puzzles or crosswords

30. Having lunch with a friend or an associate

31. Playing tennis

32. Taking a bath

33. Going for a drive

34. Woodworking

35. Writing a letter

36. Being with animals

37. Riding in an airplane

38. Walking in the woods

39. Having a conversation with someone

40. Working at your job

41. Going to a party

42. Going to church functions

43. Visiting relatives

44. Going to a meeting

45. Playing a musical instrument

46. Having a snack

47. Taking a nap

48. Singing

49. Acting

50. Working on crafts

51. Being with your children

52. Playing a game of chess or checkers

53. Putting on makeup or fixing your hair

54. Visiting people who are sick or shut in

55. Bowling

56. Talking with your sponsor

57. Gardening or doing lawn work

58. Dancing

59. Sitting in the sun

60. Sitting and thinking

61. Praying

62. Meditating

63. Listening to the sounds of nature

64. Going on a date

65. Listening to the radio

66. Giving a gift

67. Reaching out to someone who is suffering

68. Getting or giving a massage or back rub

69. Talking to your spouse

70. Talking to a friend

71. Watching the clouds

72. Lying in the grass

73. Helping someone

74. Hearing or telling jokes

75. Going to church

76. Eating a good meal

77. Hunting

78. Fishing

79. Looking at the scenery

80. Working on improving your health

81. Going downtown

82. Watching a sporting event
83. Going to a health club
84. Learning something new
85. Horseback riding
86. Going out to eat
87. Talking on the telephone
88. Daydreaming
89. Going to the movies
90. Being alone
91. Feeling the presence of God
92. Smelling a flower
93. Looking at a sunrise
94. Doing a favor for a friend
95. Meeting a stranger
96. Reading the newspaper
97. Swimming
98. Walking barefoot
99. Playing catch or with a Frisbee
100. Cleaning your house or room
101. Listening to music
102. Knitting or crocheting
103. Having house guests
104. Being with someone you love
105. Having sexual relations
106. Going to the library
107. Watching people
108. Repairing something
109. Bicycling
110. Smiling at people
111. Caring for houseplants
112. Collecting things
113. Sewing
114. Going to garage sales

115. Water skiing

116. Surfing

117. Traveling

118. Teaching someone

119. Washing your car

120. Eating ice cream

Social Skills

What you do socially can turn people off or turn them on. If you do any of the following, you might be turning people off.

1. Not smiling

2. Failing to make eye contact

3. Not talking

4. Complaining

5. Telling everyone your troubles

6. Not responding to people

7. Whining

8. Being critical

9. Poor grooming

10. Not showing interest in people

11. Ignoring people

12. Having an angry look

13. Using nervous gestures

14. Feeling sorry for yourself

15. Always talking about the negative

You are turning people on if you do the following:

1. Smiling

2. Looking at people in the eyes

3. Expressing your concern

4. Talking about pleasant things

5. Being reinforcing

6. Telling people how nice they look

7. Being appreciative

8. Telling people that you care

9. Listening

10. Touching

11. Asking people to do something with you

12. Acting interested

13. Using people's names

14. Talking about the positive

15. Grooming yourself well

To have good social skills, you have to be assertive. You cannot be passive or aggressive. This means is that you have to tell people the truth about how you feel and ask for what you want. You must tell the truth at all times. If you withhold or distort information, then you never will be close to anyone.

Do not tell other people what to do; instead, ask them what they want to do. Do not let other people tell you what to do; instead, negotiate. Do not yell; instead, explain. Do not throw your weight around. When you are wrong, promptly admit it. Happiness is giving to others. The more you give, the more you get.

In a 12-step program, you never have to be alone. Your Higher Power always is with you. Learn to enjoy the presence of God, and communicate with God as if God were standing right beside you. Call someone in the program every day. Go to many meetings. Reach out to those who are still suffering. There are many people in jails or hospitals who need your help. Volunteer to work on the 12-step hotline. Ask people out for coffee after meetings. Do not worry if you are doing all of the asking at first. The reason you are doing this is for you. Most people, particularly men, feel very uncomfortable asking others to go out with them. Do not let that stop you. If you do not ask, then you will not have the experience of someone saying yes.

Using the pleasant activities list, make a plan for how you are going to increase your social interaction this month. Write all of it down, and reward yourself when you make progress. Here are a few hints to get you going:

1. Read the activities and entertainment section of your local newspaper. Mark down events that fit into your schedule and attend them.

2. Offer to become more involved in your 12-step group.

3. Ask the local chamber of commerce for information about groups and activities in the area.

4. Spend your weekends exploring new parts of town.

5. Smile.

6. Join another self-help support group such as an Adult Children of Alcoholics group or a singles group.

7. Join a church and get involved. Tell the pastor that you want to do something to help.

8. Volunteer your services with a local charity or hospital. Help others and share your experiences, strengths, and hopes.

9. Join a group that does interesting things in the area—hiking, skydiving, hunting, bird watching, acting, playing sports, joining a senior center, and so on. Check the local library for a list of such clubs and activities.

10. Ask someone in the program for interesting things to do in the area.

11. Go to an intergroup dance.

12. Go to an Alcoholics Anonymous (AA)/Narcotics Anonymous (NA) conference.

The most important thing to remember is that you are in recovery. You are starting a new life. To do this, you must take risks. You must reach out as you have never done before.

Relapse Prevention

There is some bad news and some good news about relapse. The bad news is that many clients have problems with relapse in early sobriety. About two thirds of clients coming out of addiction programs relapse within 3 months of leaving treatment (Hunt, Barnett, & Branch, 1971). The good news is that most people who go through treatment ultimately achieve a stable recovery (Frances, Bucky, & Alexopolos, 1984). Relapse does not have to happen to you, and even if it does, you can do something about it. Relapse prevention is a daily program that can help prevent relapse. It also can stop a lapse from becoming a disaster. This exercise has been developed using a combination of the models. This uses the disease concept model in combination with motivational enhancement, cognitive behavioral therapy, skills training, and 12-step facilitation.

RELAPSE IS A PROCESS

Relapse is a process that begins long before you use drugs or alcohol. There are symptoms that precede the first use of chemicals. This exercise teaches you how to identify and control these symptoms before they lead to actual drug or alcohol use. If you allow these symptoms to go on without acting on them, then serious problems will result.

THE RELAPSE WARNING SIGNS

All relapse begins with warning signs that will signal for you that you are in trouble. If you do not recognize these signs, you will decompensate and finally use chemicals. All of the signs are a reaction to stress, and they are a reemergence of the disease. They are a means by which your body and mind are telling you that you are in trouble. You might not have all of these symptoms, but you will have some of them long before you actually use chemicals. You must determine which symptoms are the most characteristic of you, and you must come up with coping skills for dealing with each symptom.

INTERPERSONAL FACTORS

Self-efficacy is the degree you feel capable of performing a task like preventing relapse. Do you feel confident that you have the skills necessary to say no to the addiction when confronted with a high-risk situation including intense craving? Do you have the skills necessary to say no to alcohol, drugs, or addictive behavior?

Make a list of 10 things you can do when you feel craving. There are people you can call; meetings you can attend; things you can read; a Higher Power you can pray to; family members, friends, or people in the program you can share your feelings with; Alcoholics Anonymous (AA)/Narcotics Anonymous (NA)/Gamblers Anonymous (GA) hotlines you can call; physical exercise you can do; meditations you can perform, etc.

1. _____

2. _____

3. _____

4. _____

5. _____

6. _____

7. _____

8. _____

9. _____

10. _____

Practice each of these 10 things at least five times in group, with your counselor, or your sponsor/mentor/coach. You need to get used to thinking and moving in a certain way when faced with craving. If these behaviors are not practiced in stills training sessions, they are unlikely to be used when you get into trouble. Just knowing what to do is not enough; you need to practice the thoughts and motor movements to get good at the skill.

Think about the first time you learned how to ride a bike. Your teacher probably taught you all of the things you had to do to ride, but it was only after you practiced riding, repeatedly, that you began to trust yourself to ride a bike safely.

Make a list of five things in your life that you had to practice. Maybe it was basketball, baseball, soccer, or starting a conversation with someone you did not know.

1. _____

2. _____

3. _____

4. _____

5. _____

At first, you were terrible, making mostly mistakes, but after practicing thousands of times, you got better. Maybe you had to learn how to shoot a basket from the free throw line. The first times you tried, you missed most every shot. As you practiced—and particularly after you were coached—you got better. After thousands of shots, you got so you could make the shot most of the time. Then there came the big game, and the score was tied and you had to shoot the final basket. If you made the shot, your team won; if you missed the shot, you lost. Now you need to go on automatic—athletes call this getting in the zone, where all of the fans and other players disappear and it is only you and that simple shot you have practiced so many times. If you miss the shot or relapse, it is not the end of the world; it just means you need more practice until the skill becomes automatic.

Higher levels of self-efficacy predict improved addiction treatment outcomes (Burling, Reilly, Molten, & Ziff, 1989; Greenfield et al., 2000).

WHEN YOU EXPERIENCE A WARNING SIGN

When you recognize you are in trouble, you need to take action. Make a list of the coping skills you can use when you experience a high-risk situation that is common for you. It might be interpersonal conflict, anger, boredom, certain music or parts of town, seeing old friends, social pressure, negative emotions, or a celebration. This will happen. You will have high-risk situations in recovery (Marlatt & Donovan, 2008; Marlatt & Gordon, 1985). Your task is to take affirmative action. Remember, craving is a danger signal. You are in trouble. Make a list of what you are going to do. Are you going to call your sponsor, go to a meeting, call your counselor, call someone in AA/NA, tell someone, exercise, read the "Big Book" (AA, 2002), pray, become involved in an activity you enjoy, turn it over, or go into treatment? List five telephone numbers of people you can call if you are in trouble. Remember what AA says: "What we cannot do alone, we can do together."

Plan 1. _____

_____

_____

_____

_____

Plan 2. _____

_____

_____

_____

_____

Plan 3. _____

_____

_____

_____

_____

Plan 4. _____

_____

_____

_____

Plan 5. _____

_____

_____

_____

Positive Outcome Expectations

This means the positive things we think will happen if we drink or use. These are dangerous thoughts, and if not corrected, it may lead to relapse. Write down five positive thoughts about what the addiction can do for you. For example, "One drink will not hurt." "I deserve to relax with a few drinks." "I would only have one drink." "I have had a hard day." "I need to relax at the casino." "Nobody will know." "I am going to show them." "I am going to get even." "I am going to make them sorry." "I am under too much stress." "I need a break."

1. _____

2. _____

3. _____

4. _____

5. _____

Now write down 10 accurate thoughts that will keep you clean and sober. For example: "I cannot drink one drink." "I am an alcoholic." "If I start gambling I would never stop." "I would use drugs again." "I would go right back into that addiction misery again." "I can go home and talk to my wife." "I can go for a walk." "I can meditate." "I can go to a 12-step meeting." "I can call my sponsor or spiritual leader and go out for a cup of coffee." "I can read some AA/NA/GA material." "I can cope with this feeling." "If I just wait for 15 minutes, the craving will pass." "If I move away from the high-risk situation, I would feel better soon."

1. _____

2. _____

3. _____

4. _____

5. _____

6. _____

7. _____

8. _____

9. _____

10. _____

Write down these 10 alternative behaviors and carry them with you. Remember that you have to practice these skills until they become automatic. Practice saying and doing these things with your group, counselor, sponsor, mentor, coach, spouse, friend, or 12-step member. Practice, practice, practice until you feel comfortable with the new skill.

You need to check warning signs daily in your personal inventory. You also need to have other people check you daily. You will not always pick up the symptoms in yourself. You might be denying the problem again. Your spouse, your sponsor, and/or a fellow 12-step member can warn you when they believe that you might be in trouble. Listen to these people. If they tell you that they sense a problem, then take action. You might need professional help in working the problem through. Do not hesitate to call and ask for help. Anything is better than relapsing. If you overreact to a warning sign, you are not going to be in trouble. If you underreact, you might be headed for real problems. Addiction is a deadly disease. Your life is at stake.

Relapse is more likely to occur in certain situations. These situations can trigger relapse. People relapse when faced with high-risk situations that they could not cope with except by drinking or using. Your job in treatment is to develop coping skills for dealing with each high-risk situation.

Motivation

Motivation is the conscious or unconscious stimulus leading to the energy that gives you the power to act. Either you can act in an adaptive or a maladaptive way; both can be positive or negative reinforcers. You can have motivation to stay clean and sober, and you can have motivation to return to your addiction.

Prochaska and DiClemente (1984) proposed a model for motivation that goes through five stages or readiness for change: (1) precontemplation, (2) contemplation, (3) preparation, (4) action, and (5) maintenance. Each stage characterizes a different level of motivational readiness for change.

- Interventions that cause ambivalence, evaluating the pros and cons of change, may increase motivation by allowing clients to explore their own morals and values and how they may differ if they institute change. For example, people who are in the precontemplative stage have no interest in behavior change. If they explore the pros and cons of the addictive behavior, they might become more willing to think about the positive aspects of changing.
- This moves them into contemplation, where you discuss all of the positive and negative aspects of using or stopping the addiction. Once the decision is made to try to stop the addictive behavior then we must concentrate on what needs to change to stop the addictive behavior.
- Then the action phase begins where we begin to change the thoughts and behaviors that cause addiction.
- Once the addiction stops then we need skills to maintain this new lifestyle.

Negative Emotions

Many people relapse when feeling negative feelings that they cannot cope with. Most feel angry or frustrated, but some feel anxious, bored, lonely, or depressed. Almost any negative feeling can lead to relapse if you do not learn how to cope with the feeling. Feelings motivate you to take action. You must act to solve any problem.

Circle any of the following feelings that seem to lead you to use chemicals.

1. Loneliness
2. Anger
3. Rejection
4. Emptiness
5. Annoyed
6. Sad
7. Exasperated
8. Betrayed
9. Cheated
10. Frustrated
11. Envious
12. Exhausted
13. Bored
14. Anxious
15. Ashamed
16. Bitter
17. Burdened
18. Foolish
19. Jealous
20. Left out
21. Selfish
22. Restless
23. Weak
24. Sorrowful
25. Greedy
26. Aggravated
27. Manipulated
28. Miserable
29. Unloved

30. Worried

31. Scared

32. Spiteful

33. Sorrowful

34. Helpless

35. Neglected

36. Grief

37. Confused

38. Crushed

39. Discontented

40. Restless

41. Irritated

42. Overwhelmed

43. Panicked

44. Trapped

45. Unsure

46. Intimidated

47. Distraught

48. Uneasy

49. Guilty

50. Threatened

A Plan to Deal With Negative Emotions

These are just a few of the feeling words. Add more if you need to do so. Develop coping skills for dealing with each feeling that makes you vulnerable to relapse. Exactly what are you going to do when you have this feeling? Detail your specific plan of action. Some options are talking to your sponsor, calling a friend in the program, going to a meeting, calling your counselor, reading some recovery material, turning it over to your Higher Power, and getting some exercise. For each feeling, develop a specific plan of action.

Feeling _____

Plan 1. _____

Plan 2. _____

Plan 3. _____

Feeling _____

Plan 1. _____

Plan 2. _____

Plan 3. _____

Feeling _____

Plan 1. _____

Plan 2. _____

Plan 3. _____

Continue to fill out these feeling forms until you have all of the feelings that give you trouble and you have coping skills for dealing with each feeling.

Social Pressure

Social pressure can be direct (where someone directly encourages you to use chemicals) or indirect (a social situation where people are using). Both of these situations can trigger intense craving, and this can lead to relapse. More than 60% of alcoholics relapse in bars.

Certain friends are more likely to encourage you to use chemicals. These people do not want to hurt you. They want you to relax and have a good time. They want their old friend back. They do not understand the nature of your disease. Perhaps they are chemically dependent themselves and are in denial.

High-Risk Friends

Make a list of the friends who might encourage you to use drugs or alcohol.

1. _____

2. _____

3. _____

4. _____

5. _____

What are you going to do when they offer you drugs? What are you going to say? In group, set up a situation where the whole group encourages you to use chemicals. Look carefully at how you feel when the group members are encouraging you. Look at what you say. Have them help you to develop appropriate ways of saying no. The skills of saying no are the following:

- Look at the person, and say no thank you.
- Suggest another alternative behavior.
- If the person persists, tell them that you are trying to stop behavior that has been harming you. Then ask them to help you by respecting your choice not to use.
- If they persist, leave the situation. "Well, I have got to be going. Nice to see you."

High-Risk Social Situations

Certain social situations will trigger craving. These are the situations where you have used chemicals in the past. Certain bars or restaurants, a particular part of town, certain music, athletic events, parties, weddings, and family events—all of these situations can trigger intense cravings. Make a list of five social situations where you will be vulnerable to relapse.

1. _____

2. _____

3. _____

4. _____

5. _____

In early sobriety, you will need to avoid these situations and friends. To put yourself in a high-risk situation is asking for trouble. If you have to attend a function where there will be people using chemicals, then take someone with you who is in the program. Take someone with you who will support you in your sobriety. Make sure that you have a way to get home. You do not have to stay and torture yourself. You can leave if you feel uncomfortable. Avoid all situations where your sobriety feels shaky.

Interpersonal Conflict

Many addicts relapse when in a conflict with some other person. They have a problem with someone and have no idea of how to cope with conflict so they might revert to old behavior and use the addiction to deal with the uncomfortable feelings. The stress of the problem builds and leads to using. This conflict usually happens with someone who they are closely involved with—wife, husband, child, parent, sibling, friend, boss, and so on.

You can have a serious problem with anyone—even a stranger—so you must have a plan for dealing with interpersonal conflict. You will develop specific skills in treatment that will help you to communicate even when you are under stress.

You need to learn and practice the following interpersonal skills repeatedly.

1. Tell the truth all the time.

2. Share how you feel.

3. Ask for what you want.

4. Find some truth in what the other person is saying.

5. Be willing to compromise.

If you can stay in the conflict and work it out, great. If you cannot, then you have to leave the situation and take care of yourself. You might have to go for a walk, a run, or a drive. You might need to cool down. You must stop the conflict. You cannot continue to try to deal with a situation that you believe is too much for you. Do not feel bad about this. Interpersonal relationships are the hardest challenge we face. Carry a card with you that has the telephone numbers of people who you can contact. You might want to call your sponsor, minister, or counselor or a fellow AA/NA/GA member, friend, family member, doctor, or anyone else who may support you.

In an interpersonal conflict, you will fear abandonment. You need to get accurate and reassure yourself that people can disagree with you and still care about you. Remember that your Higher Power cares about you. A Higher Power created you and loves you. Remember the other people in your life who love you. This is one of the main reasons for talking with someone else. When the other person listens to you that person gives you the feeling that you are accepted and loved.

If you still feel afraid or angry, then get with someone you trust and stay with that person until you feel safe. Do not struggle out there all by yourself. Any member of your 12-step group will understand how you are feeling. We all have had these problems. We all have felt lost, helpless, hopeless, and angry.

Make an emergency card that lists all of the people who you can call if you are having difficulty. Write down their phone numbers, and carry this card with you at all times. Show this card to your counselor. Practice asking someone for help in treatment once each day. Write down the situation and show it to your counselor. Get into the habit of asking for help. When you get out of treatment, call someone every day just to stay in touch and keep the lines of communication open. Get used to it. Do not wait to ask for help at the last minute. This makes asking more difficult.

Positive Feelings

Some people relapse when they are feeling positive emotions. Think of all the times you used drugs and alcohol to celebrate. That has gotten to be such a habit that when something good happens you will immediately think about using. You need to be ready when you feel like a winner. This may be at a wedding, birth, promotion, or any event where you feel good. How are you going to celebrate without drugs and alcohol? Make a celebration plan. You might have to take someone with you to a celebration, particularly in early recovery.

Positive feelings also can work when you are by yourself. A beautiful spring day can be enough to get you thinking about drinking or using. You need an action plan for when these thoughts pass through your mind. You must immediately get accurate and get real. In recovery, we are committed to reality. Do not sit there and recall how wonderful you will feel if you get high. Tell yourself the truth. Think about all of the pain that addiction has caused you. If you toy with positive feelings, then you ultimately will use chemicals.

Circle the positive feelings that may make you vulnerable to relapse.

1. Affection

2. Boldness

3. Braveness

4. Calmness

5. Capableness

6. Cheerfulness

7. Confidence

8. Delightfulness

9. Desire

10. Enchantment

11. Joy

12. Freeness

13. Gladness

14. Glee

15. Happiness

16. Honor

17. Horny

18. Infatuation

19. Inspired

20. Kinky

21. Lazy

22. Loving

23. Peaceful

24. Pleasant

25. Pleased

26. Sexy

27. Wonderful

28. Cool

29. Relaxed

30. Reverent

31. Silly

32. Vivacious

33. Adequate

34. Efficient

35. Successful

36. Accomplished

37. Hopeful

38. Cheery

39. Elated

40. Merry

41. Ecstatic

42. Upbeat

43. Splendid

44. Yearning

45. Bliss

46. Excitement

47. Exhilaration

48. Proudness

49. Aroused

50. Festive

Plans to Cope With Positive Feelings

These are the feelings that may make you vulnerable to relapse. You must be careful when you are feeling good because pleasure triggers the same part of the brain that triggers addiction. Make an action plan for dealing with each positive emotion that makes you vulnerable to using chemicals.

Feeling _____

Plan 1. _____

Plan 2. _____

Plan 3. _____

Feeling _____

Plan 1. _____

Plan 2. _____

Plan 3. _____

Feeling _____

Plan 1. _____

Plan 2. _____

Plan 3. _____

Continue this planning until you develop a plan for each of the positive feelings that make you vulnerable. Practice what you are going to do when you experience positive feelings.

Test Control

Some people relapse to test whether they can use the addiction again. They fool themselves into thinking that they might be able to use normally. This time they will use only a little. This time they will be able to stay in control of themselves. People who fool themselves this way are in for big trouble. From the first use, most people are in full-blown relapse within 30 days.

Testing personal control begins with inaccurate thinking. It takes you back to Step One. You need to think accurately. You are powerless over mood-altering chemicals. If you use, then you will lose. It is as simple as that. You are physiologically, psychologically, and socially addicted. The cells in your body will not suddenly change no matter how long you are clean and sober. You are chemically dependent in your cells. This never will change.

How to See Through the First Use

You need to look at how the illness part of yourself will try to convince you that you are not chemically dependent. The illness will flash on the screen of your consciousness all the good things that the addiction did for you. Make a list of these things. In the first column, marked "Early Use," write down some of the good things that you were getting out of using chemicals. Why were you using? What good came out of it? Did it make you feel social, smart, pretty, intelligent, brave, popular, desirable, relaxed, or sexy? Did it help you to sleep? Did it make you feel confident? Did it help you to forget your problems? Make a long list. These are the good things that you were getting when you first started using. This is why you were using.

Early Use	Late Use
1.	1.
2.	2.
3.	3.
4.	4.
5.	5.
6.	6.
7.	7.
8.	8.
9.	9.
10.	10.

Now go back and place in the second column, marked "Late Use," how you were doing in that area once you became addicted. How were you doing in that same area right before you came into treatment? Did you still feel social, or did you feel alone? Did you still feel intelligent, or did you feel stupid? You will find that a great change has taken place. The very things that you were using for in early use you get the opposite of in late use. If you were drinking for sleep, then you cannot sleep. If you were using to be more popular, then you are more isolated, insecure, and alone. If you were using to feel brave, then you are feeling more afraid. This is a major characteristic of addiction. The good things you got at first you get the opposite of in addiction. You can never go back to early use because your brain has permanently changed in chemistry, structure, and genetics.

Take a long look at both of these lists, and think about how the illness is going to try to work inside of your thinking. The addicted part of yourself will present to you all of the good things you got in early use. This is how the disease will encourage you to use. You must see through the first use to the consequences that are dead ahead.

Look at that second list. You must see the misery that is coming if you use chemicals. For most people who relapse, there are only a few days of controlled use before loss of control sets in. There usually are only a few hours or days before all of the bad stuff begins to click back into place. Relapse is terrible. It is the most intense misery that you can imagine.

Lapse and Relapse

A lapse is the use of any addictive substance or behavior. A relapse is continuing to use the behavior until the full biological, psychological, and social disease is present. All of the complex biological, psychological, and social components of the disease become evident very quickly.

The Lapse Plan

You must have a plan in case you lapse. It is foolish to think that you never will have a problem again. You must plan what you are going to do if you have a problem. Hunt et al. (1971), in a study of recovering addicts, found that 33% of clients lapsed within 2 weeks of leaving treatment, and 60% lapsed within 3 months. At the end of 8 months, 63% had used. At the end of 12 months, 67% had used.

The worst thing you can do when you have a lapse is to think that you have completely failed in recovery. This is inaccurate thinking. You are not a total failure. You have not lost everything. A lapse is a great learning opportunity. You have made a mistake, and you can learn from it. You let some part of your program go, and you are paying for it. You need to examine exactly what happened and get back into recovery.

A lapse is an emergency. It is a matter of life or death. You must take immediate action to prevent the lapse from becoming a full relapse. You must call someone in the program—preferably your sponsor—and tell that person what happened. You need to examine why you had a problem. You cannot use the addiction and the tools of recovery at the same time. Something went wrong. You did not use your new skills. You must make a plan of action to recover from your lapse. You cannot do this by yourself. You are in denial. You do not know the whole truth. If you did, you would not have relapsed.

Call your sponsor or a professional counselor, and have that person develop a new treatment plan for you. You may need to attend more meetings. You may need to see a counselor. You may need outpatient treatment. You may need inpatient treatment.

You have to get honest with yourself. You need to develop a plan and follow it. You need someone else to agree to keep an eye on you for a while. Do not try to do this alone. What we cannot do alone, we can do together.

THE BEHAVIOR CHAIN

All behavior occurs in a certain sequence. First, there is the *trigger*. This is the external event that starts the behavioral sequence. After the trigger, there comes *thinking*. Much of this thinking is very fast, and you will not consciously pick it up unless you stop and think about it. The thoughts trigger *feeling*, which gives you energy and direction for action. Next comes the *behavior* or the action initiated by the trigger. Lastly, there always is a *consequence* for any action.

Diagrammed, the behavior chain looks like this:

Trigger → Thinking → Feeling → Behavior → Consequence

Let us go through a behavioral sequence and see how it works. On the way home from work, Bob, a recovering alcoholic, passes the local bar. (This is the trigger.) He thinks, "I have had a hard day. I need a couple of beers to unwind." (The trigger initiates thinking.) Bob craves a beer. (The thinking initiates feeling.) Bob turns into the bar and begins drinking. (The feeling initiates behavior.) Bob relapses. (The behavior has a consequence.)

Let us work through another example. It is 11:00 pm, and Bob is not asleep (trigger). He thinks, "I would never get to sleep tonight unless I have a few drinks" (thinking). He feels an increase in his anxiety about not sleeping (feeling). He gets up and consumes a few drinks (behavior). He gets drunk and wakes up hungover and unable to work the next morning (consequence).

How to Cope With Triggers

At every point along the behavior chain, you can work on preventing relapse. First, you need to carefully examine your triggers. What environmental events lead you to using chemicals? We went over some of these when we examined high-risk situations. Determine what people, places, or things make you vulnerable to relapse. Stay away from these triggers as much as possible. If a trigger occurs, then use your new coping skills.

Do not let the trigger initiate old behavior. Stop and think. Do not let your thinking get out of control. Challenge your thinking and get accurate about what is real. Let us look at some common inaccurate thoughts.

1. It is not going to hurt.

2. No one is going to know.

3. I need to relax.

4. I am just going to have a couple.

5. I have had a hard day.

6. My friends want me to drink.

7. I never had a problem with pot.

8. It is the only way I can sleep.

9. I can do anything I want to.

10. I am lonely.

All of these inaccurate thoughts can be used to fuel the craving that leads to relapse. You must stop and challenge your thinking until you are thinking accurately. You must replace inaccurate thoughts with accurate ones. You are chemically dependent. If you drink or use drugs, then you will die. That is the truth. Think through the first drink. Get honest with yourself.

How to Cope With Craving

If you think inaccurately, then you will begin craving. This is the powerful feeling that drives compulsive drug use. Craving is like an ocean wave; it will build and then wash over you. Craving does not last long if you move away from your drug of choice. If you move closer to the drug, then the craving will increase until you are compelled to use. Immediately on feeling a desire to use, think this thought:

"Drinking/Drug use/Gambling is no longer an option for me."

Now drinking and using drugs no longer is an option. What are your options? You are in trouble. You are craving. What are you going to do to prevent relapse? You must move away from your drug of choice. Perhaps you need to call your sponsor, go to a meeting, turn it over, call the AA/NA/GA hotline, call the treatment center, call your counselor, go for a walk, run, or visit someone. You must do something else other than think about chemicals. Do not sit there and ponder using. You will lose that debate. This illness is called the great debater. If you leave it unchecked, it will seduce you into using chemicals.

Remember that the illness must lie to work. You must uncover the lie as quickly as possible and get back to the truth. You must take the appropriate action necessary to maintain your sobriety.

A DAILY RELAPSE PREVENTION PLAN

If you work a daily program of recovery, then your chances of success increase greatly. You need to evaluate your recovery daily and keep a log. This is your daily inventory.

1. Assess all relapse warning signs.
   a. What symptoms did I see in myself today?
   b. What am I going to do about them?

2. Assess love of self.
   a. What did I do to love myself today?
   b. What am I going to do tomorrow?

3. Assess love of others.
   a. What did I do to love others today?
   b. What am I going to do tomorrow?

4. Assess love of God.

   a. What did I do to love God today?

   b. What am I going to do tomorrow?

5. Assess sleep pattern.

   How am I sleeping?

6. Assess exercise.

   Am I getting enough exercise?

7. Assess nutrition.

   Am I eating right?

8. Review total recovery program.

   a. How am I doing in recovery?

   b. What is the next step in my recovery program?

9. Read *24 Hours a Day* (Walker, 1992).

10. Make conscious contact with God.

    a. Pray and meditate for a few minutes.

    b. Relax completely.

Social Support System

Every client needs to build a social support system. Positive social support is highly predictive of long-term abstinence rates across many addictive behaviors. You need to write down specifically who is going to be your advocate at home, work, community, and school. This person needs to talk to your counselor and understand exactly what being an advocate means. This person will have different tasks depending upon whether or not he or she is a schoolteacher, parent, spouse, pastor, sponsor, mentor, coach, community leader, school counselor, doctor, nurse, counselor, etc. You need to make a list of all of these people and decide who is going to do what. Someone needs to run up to three urine drug screens every week for the first 6 months and up to one drug screen a week for the next 5 years. This best person for this is the continuing care case manager. The client calls in every morning to see if this is one of the drug testing days or not. If so, the client goes to the clinic and gives a urine sample.

PEOPLE WHO CAN HELP YOU IN RECOVERY

1. Case Manager: _____ Phone: _____

The continuing care case manager makes sure everyone on the team is working together to keep the client clean and sober. This person keeps a record of all therapy meetings, 12-step groups, and drug screens. He or she has a contract with the client that outlines exactly what is expected of the client and what the consequences are if the client does not follow through with the recovery program.

2. Parent or Spouse: _____ Phone: _____

    The parent or spouse will be the person who knows what behavior is adaptive and maladaptive. What friends are to be avoided? If an adolescent develops the behavioral contract, he or she is responsible for rewards and consequences.

3. The Teacher: _____ Phone: _____

    Employer: _____ Phone: _____

    Everyone on the team knows about what behavior is to be expected and what is not to be tolerated. Members of the team often call each other to check up on the facts and make sure everyone is on the same page.

4. The Sponsor/Mentor/Coach: _____ Phone: _____

    The sponsor, mentor, or coach is the person who guides the client through recovery. They have been or are in a 12-step program themselves and take the client to meetings and meet regularly to discuss the recovery process.

5. The Physician: _____ Phone: _____

    The physician orders the medication and does history and physical examinations to maintain good health.

6. The Spiritual Guide: _____ Phone: _____

    The spiritual guide helps the patient discuss and grow in his or her spiritual journey. The client shares his or her spiritual journey and maybe keeps a spiritual prayer journal.
    Fill out this inventory every day following treatment, and keep a journal about how you are doing. You will be amazed as you read back over your journal from time to time. You will be surprised at how much you have grown.
    Make a list of 10 reasons why you want to stay clean and sober.

    1. _____

    2. _____

    3. _____

    4. _____

    5. _____

    6. _____

7. _____

8. _____

9. _____

10. _____

Never forget these reasons. Read this list over and over to yourself. Carry a copy with you and memorize them. If you are struggling in sobriety, then take it out and read it to yourself. You are important. No one has to live a life of misery. You can recover and live a clean and sober life.

I am in the _____.

_____ Precontemplation stage

_____ Contemplation stage

_____ Preparation stage

_____ Action stage

_____ Maintenance stage

Personal Recovery Plan

Name: _____   Home Phone:_____

Admission Date: _____   Work Phone: _____

Discharge Date: _____

Name of Significant Other: _____   Phone:_____

It is important to your recovery to continue to work through your problems on discharge. Your recovery never can stand still. You must be constantly moving forward in your program. Working with your counselor, you must detail exactly what you need to do following inpatient treatment. Each psychological problem or family problem will need a specific plan of action. You must commit yourself to following this recovery plan to the letter. Do not think that just because you have completed treatment that your problems are over. Your recovery is just beginning, and you need to work diligently to stay clean and sober.

Make a list of the problems that you need to address in continuing care. Any emotional, family, legal, social, physical, leisure, work, spiritual, or school problem will have to have a plan. How are you going to address that problem in recovery? What is the goal? What do you want to achieve? Develop your personal recovery plan with your counselor's assistance.

A. Treatment plan for continued sobriety

   1. Problem 1: _____

      Goal: _____

      Plan: _____

      _____

      _____

2. Problem 2: _____

   Goal: _____

   Plan: _____

      _____

      _____

3. Problem 3: _____

   Goal: _____

   Plan: _____

      _____

      _____

4. Problem 4: _____

   Goal: _____

   Plan: _____

      _____

      _____

5. Problem 5: _____

   Goal: _____

   Plan: _____

      _____

      _____

B. Relapse

In the event of a relapse, list five steps that you will take to deal with the problem.

1. _____

2. _____

3. _____

4. _____

5. _____

C. Support in recovery

Indicate the 12-step meetings that you will attend each week after discharge. We recommend that you attend 90 meetings in 90 days at first and at least 3 to 5 meetings per week for the remainder of that year, and then you can attend once a week for at least the next 5 years.

Day:_____

Time:_____

Location:_____

D. Indicate when you will attend the continuing care group.

Day: _____

Time: _____

Location: _____

E. Who are three 12-step contact persons who can provide you with support in early recovery?

Name: _____ Phone: _____

Name: _____ Phone: _____

Name: _____ Phone: _____

F. If you have any problems or concerns in sobriety, you always can call the treatment center staff at the following number:

Counselor: _____

Phone: _____

G. If you and your counselor have arranged for further counseling or treatment following discharge, then complete the following:

Name of Agency:

Address: _____ Phone: _____

_____

_____

First Appointment:_____

Day:_____

Time:_____

H. List 10 things that you are going to do daily to stay clean and sober.

1. _____

2. _____

3. _____

4. _____

5. _____

6. _____

7. _____

8. _____

9. _____

10. _____

I. You are changing your lifestyle. It will be important to avoid certain people and situations that will put you at high risk. List 10 people and places you need to avoid in early recovery.

1. _____

2. _____

3. _____

4. _____

5. _____

6. _____

7. _____

8. _____

9. _____

10. _____

You will need a series of advocates who know your story and commitment to stay clean and sober. You sign a release with each of these people so they can talk to each other about your recovery. It helps to have someone at home, work, school, and community. List their names and numbers, contact them, and ask them to be an advocate for you in your community.

• Home Advocate:

Person: _____ Phone: _____ Address: _____

_____

_____

- School Advocate:

Person: _____Phone:_____Address: _____

_____

_____

- Work Advocate:

Person: _____Phone:_____Address: _____

_____

_____

Community Advocate:

Person: _____Phone:_____Address: _____

_____

_____

Case Manager:

Person: _____Phone:_____Address: _____

_____

_____

You will call the case manager every day to see if this is a day for you to come in for drug testing. You will get up to three drug tests per week for the first 6 months and up to one drug test for the next 5 years. You will send in a monthly log of 12-step meetings to your case manager by the 10th of each month. Each meeting has to be dated and signed by the meeting leader. The case manager will receive reports from all of the treatment that was recommended by the treatment center, such as anger management, marriage counseling, etc. You will sign a contract with the case manager that gives consequences if you do not follow the continuing care program. This will mean the manager will contact your boss, probation officer, family members, licensing board, or another person or agency that is dedicated to your successful treatment.

STATEMENT OF COMMITMENT

I understand that the success of my recovery depends on adherence to my recovery plan. The continuing care program has been explained to me, and I understand fully what I must do in recovery. I commit to myself that I will follow this plan.

    With your continuing care manager, write out your continuing care plan and then have all mentors/sponsors/coaches and advocates sign it.

Client Signature: _____

Physician Signature: _____

Sponsor Signature: _____

Employer Signature: _____

Significant Other Signature: _____

Licensing Board Signature: _____

Community Advocate Signature: _____

School Advocate Signature: _____

Case Manager Signature: _____

Counselor Signature: _____

Date: _____

Appendix

Daily Craving Record

Rate your cravings every day on a scale of 0 (the least amount of craving possible) to 10 (the most craving possible). Then put down the situation or thoughts that triggered the craving. Have your counselor or group help you uncover the automatic thoughts or situations that triggered craving. Do this at least for the first 90 days of recovery. Make as many copies of these pages that you need. In treatment, you will replace inaccurate thoughts with accurate thoughts.

0 = No craving   3 = moderate craving   10 = severe craving

Date ___ Craving ___ Triggers _____

Date ___ Craving ___ Triggers _____

Date ___ Craving ___ Triggers _____

Date ___ Craving ___ Triggers _____

Date ___ Craving ___ Triggers _____

Date ___ Craving ___ Triggers _____

Date ___ Craving ___ Triggers _____

Date ___ Craving ___ Triggers _____

Date ___ Craving ___ Triggers _____

Date ___ Craving ___ Triggers _____

Date ___ Craving ___ Triggers _____

Date ___ Craving ___ Triggers _____

Date ___ Craving ___ Triggers _____

Date ___ Craving ___ Triggers _____

Date ___ Craving ___ Triggers _____

Date ___ Craving ___ Triggers _____

Date ___ Craving ___ Triggers _____

Date ___ Craving ___ Triggers _____

Date ___ Craving ___ Triggers _____

Date ___ Craving ___ Triggers _____

Date ___ Craving ___ Triggers _____

Date ___ Craving ___ Triggers _____

Date ___ Craving ___ Triggers _____

Date ___ Craving ___ Triggers _____

Date ___ Craving ___ Triggers _____

Date ___ Craving ___ Triggers _____

Date ___ Craving ___ Triggers _____

Date ___ Craving ___ Triggers _____

Date ___ Craving ___ Triggers _____

Date ___ Craving ___ Triggers _____

Date ___ Craving ___ Triggers _____

Date ___ Craving ___ Triggers _____

Date ___ Craving ___ Triggers _____

Date ___ Craving ___ Triggers _____

Date ___ Craving ___ Triggers _____

Date ___ Craving ___ Triggers _____

Date ___ Craving ___ Triggers _____

Date ___ Craving ___ Triggers _____

Date ___ Craving ___ Triggers _____

Date ___ Craving ___ Triggers _____

Date ___ Craving ___ Triggers _____

Date ___ Craving ___ Triggers _____

Date ___ Craving ___ Triggers _____

References

Alcoholics Anonymous. (2001). *Alcoholics Anonymous*. New York: Alcoholics Anonymous World Services.

Alcoholics Anonymous. (2002). *Twelve steps and twelve traditions*. New York: Alcoholics Anonymous World Services.

Burling, T. A., Reilly, P. M, Molten, J. O., & Ziff, D. C. (1989). Self-efficacy and relapse among imclient drug and alcohol abusers: A predictior of outcome. *Journal of Studed on Alcohol*, *50*(4), 354–360.

Frances, R. J., Bucky, S., & Alexopolos, G. S. (1984). Outcome study of familial and nonfamilial alcoholism. *American Journal of Psychiatry*, *141*, 11.

Greenfield, S., Hufford, M., Vagge, L., Muenz, L., Costello, M., & Weiss, R. (2000). The relationship of self-efficacy expectations to relapse among alcohol dependent men and women: A prospective study. *Journal of Studies on Alcohol*, *61*, 345–351.

Hunt, W. A., Barnett. L. W., & Branch, L. G. (1971). Relapse rates in addiction programs. *Journal of Clinical Psychology*, *27*, 455–456.

Marlatt, A. G., & Donovan, D. M. (Eds.). (2008). *Relapse prevention: Maintenance strategies in the treatment of addictive behaviors*. New York: Guilford Press.

Marlatt, A. G., & Gordon, J. R. (1985). *Relapse prevention*. New York: Guilford Press.

Narcotics Anonymous. (1988). *Narcotics Anonymous*. Van Nuys, CA: Narcotics Anonymous World Service Office.

Prochaska, J. O., & DiClemente, C. C. (1984). *The transtheoretical approach: Crossing the traditional boundaries of therapy*. Malabar, FL: Krieger.

Walker, R. (1992). *Twenty-four hours a day*. Center City, MN: Hazelden.

About the Author

Robert R. Perkinson is the clinical director of Keystone Treatment Center in Canton, South Dakota. He is a licensed psychologist; licensed marriage & family therapist; internationally certified alcohol and drug counselor; South Dakota certified chemical dependency counselor, Level III; and a nationally certified gambling counselor and supervisor. His specialty areas focus on treating alcoholics, addicts, and pathological gamblers. He is the author of *Chemical Dependency Counseling: A Practical Guide* (2nd ed.) (2003a), which is the leading treatment manual in the world for chemical dependency counselors. With Dr. Arthur E. Jongsma Jr. (2001) he is the coauthor of *The Addiction Treatment Planner*, which is the best-selling treatment planner and computer software program for mental health and addiction professionals. He has also written *The Alcoholism and Drug Abuse Patient Workbook* (2003c) and the *Gambling Addiction Patient Workbook* (2003b). These workbooks have all of the exercises patients need to enter a stable recovery. His book entitled *Treating Alcoholism: How to Help Your Clients Enter Recovery* (2004) trains professionals how to treat patients with alcohol problems. He is the author of the book *God Talks to You* (2000) and the meditation tape *A Communication from God* (2008) by cdbaby, which help addicts make their first conscious contact with a Higher Power of their own understanding. He is a composer and has completed his second CD, *Peace Will Come*, music that helps addicts learn the essentials of a spiritual journey. With Dr. Jean LaCour (2004), he wrote the *Faith-Based Addiction Curriculum* to teach professionals of faith how to treat addiction. Dr. Perkinson is an international motivational speaker and regular contributor to numerous professional journals. He is the webmaster of several web pages, including www .robertperkinson.com, www.alcoholismtreatment.org, and www.godtalkstoyou.com, where he gets over 2.6 million hits a year and answers questions on addiction for free. His biographies can be found in *Who's Who in America, Who's Who in Medicine and Healthcare, Who's Who in Science and Engineering,* and *Who's Who in the World.*